PICTURES ON FRONT COVER

Left to right back row
Fredrick D.B. Weathersby, Trinity N. Weathersby, Jaryn J. Rowland,
Marcus D. Lewis, Evan W. Weathersby

Left to right front Row
Emmanuel N. Weathersby, Sylvanus P. Weathersby IV,
Jace Michael(Short Stop) Green, DeBorah McFadden-Rowland,
Al Hajji Robert J. Rowland, LeAndra (LeLe) R. Sledge and
Charlotte McFadden-Ladd

Theola McFadden and Fred McFadden

Uncle Dr. Calvin O. Atchison, DeBorah McFadden-Rowland and
Al Hajji Robert J.- Rowland.

First Lady Ella Clay, DeBorah McFadden-Rowland,
Al Hajji Robert J Rowland and Pastor Glenn V. Clay

Flo Rowland and Robert Rowland Sr.

Blending of the Family Pebbles Ceremony
DeBorah McFadden Rowland – Al Hajji Robert J. Rowland

Trey Dowling, Debra Rowland-Washington,
DeBorah McFadden Rowland, AL Hajji Robert J. Rowland and
LeAndra (LeLe) R. Sledge

Photos provided by Evan Weathersby@ Weathersby Imagery

Your Gift Will Make Room

For You

Al Hajji Robert J. Rowland

ISBN: Softcover   978-0-692-65674-7
Jabil Anur Records And Publishing

This is a work of fiction. Names, characters, places and incidents
either are the product of the author's imagination or are used
fictitiously, and any resemblance to any actual persons, living or
dead, events, or locales is entirely coincidental.
This Book was printed in the United States of America.

Contents

Poems, Songs and Inspirations

Contents

Contents

Forward

Al Hajji Robert J. Rowland, began writing and compiling this book of poetry, songs, food for thought, famous quotes and Nannyism's around 2011. As ideas came to him, he wrote them down. He really became motivated to complete this work in Mayfield, Kentucky during the time when he was taking care of his beloved mother (Nanny) during the last two years and nine months of her life. His creative energy can be experienced as you read through the pages of this unique work of literature. His gift of writing has made room for him to educate, enlighten and inspire others to think, do research and learn.

DeBorah McFadden-Rowland

Dedication

I would like to dedicate this book to my biological children LeAndra (LeLe), Rakiem (Roc), Tamika and Jaryn(Isa) and my grandson LaDamien. You are all special and wonderful in your own unique way. May God continue to bless each of you in your endeavors. Just let the record show that I love you all dearly and the moments we have spent together will always be special. May you continue to let your gifts and talents make room for you. To my wife DeBorah McFadden-Rowland and her sons Sylvanus IV, Fredrick, Emmanuel, Evan and her daughter Trinity as well as grandson, Jace (Short Stop) who have embraced me. Let the love flow in our family blending and our God will sit at the head of the table in this union. I also would like to give a special dedication to my lost relatives from Ancient Kemit (Egypt) in Africa who practiced the Maathian Creed a natural spiritual consciousness that kept us in tune with life and the rhythm of the universe based on the Cosmic Natural Law of Maat (Truth, Justice, Peace, Wisdom and Love) and to Dad and Nanny Rowland, Fred and Theola McFadden, rest in peace, love you and miss you.

AL Hajji Robert J. Rowland

Food For Thought

May the light of God shine on our Souls
And may the mercy of God envelope mankind
And heal us of our past transgressions.

Al Hajji Robert J. Rowland

About The Author

Robert J. Rowland, A.K.A. (Squirrelly) Al Hajji Omowalle Alif Abdul Rakiem, which means the first son who has returned home, a servant of God, the writer, who has made a pilgrimage to the Holy City of Mecca, Saudi Arabia. Al Hajji the poet, songwriter and author was born in Mayfield, Kentucky and raised in East Palo Alto, California. He now resides in Nashville, Tennessee. He has a Bachelor of Science in Business Management from Mid-Continent University. Mr. Rowland left the Bay Area, after high school and attended Cal State University Fullerton, and transferred to Tennessee State University in Nashville, Tennessee on a baseball scholarship. At TSU, he developed his poetry and songwriting skills and was a member of the Natural Experience singing group, where he played percussion. He also co-founded the Poets and Songwriters Association of TSU, which is still a charter organization on campus. Al Hajji became a member of the Total Experience Record Company in 1980 where he signed an artist and songwriting contract. There he befriended the Gap Band (Charlie, Ronnie & Robert Wilson R.I.P.), Yarborough & Peoples, Val Young, Raymond Calhoun, and Lonnie Simmons as well as Don Alexander the owners. Over the years he has been active in the music industry giving workshops on writing and the business end of music. Singing at weddings and receptions and working with Alicia Cherry as a personal manager, where he became friends with the late Lisa (Left Eye) Nicole Lopes (N.I.N.A.) Raina Reigndrop Lopes, Kisha Spivey of the group Total and the Girl group Ejypt (Joy, Katrina, Temel & Sophia). Al Hajji has published two other books entitled "On The Mountain Of Light" and "From The Hood To The Holy Land And Back Plus More". The books are available through Xlibris.com, Amazon.com and your local book stores.
May God have mercy on our world and let there be peace.

Key To The Universe

God Is supreme. He is over us all,

Just like a stream that fresh water flows down,

He is always around us inside our hearts.

Has faith escaped your upbringing? Or do you really care?

One love, one God, is that not what the Messiah taught us?

Look into your soul rich man if you are greedy.

Will you be able to cross over to the right side?

Even though despair is in our poor communities,

do we have to kill, sell dope and have gang war-fare?

The Prophets came to warn us,

When God was not in mankind hearts,

wisdom is the key to life in our universe.

Food For Thought

Man, made religions have blinded the human race from true
brotherhood.
Maat will rise again from the primeval mound where creation began.
One God love! Peace will reign, supreme one day at a time!

Al Hajji Robert J. Rowland

The Champion

You were my hero, my Pharaoh, the Sampson of your time.
God had blessed you to fight inside and outside the ring.
You were a warner to wake up the mind of a people.
Who were wrongly submitted to injustices, by a democratic regime
in the disguise of Nazism. Rural America we are in the 21st
Century, living in one of the greatest societies on earth. The Papyrus
of Ani, Lotus Sutra Majjima Nikaya, Bible, Koran, Shruti, Nag
Hammadi, Circle 7 Koran and Torah all say love your brother and
neighbors regardless of their color. Thank you again for being the
greatest, you floated like a butterfly and stung like a bee. You stood
up for justice, equality, freedom and human rights.
You would not go fight a war, in some foreign land.
There were plenty of battles, right here in America then
trying to change Racism into Humanism.
The war was against the hierarchy in Washington, D.C.
The people's voices were shouting with new ideologies.
Was Islam a reason for being a conscientious objector
Against a war in Vietnam?
Was it not true that African Americans were second class
citizen fighting for dignity, citizenship and the abolishment of Jim
Crow? Who said that separate but equal was fair? Muhammad Ali
we love you for your stand. Thank you for showing a generation on
how to be Men.

Dedicated to Muhammad Ali

That Place

Look up baby there is the morning Star.

I am so happy that love found us again.

No More Pain in our lives.

Only the Joy of God Love.

We have taken many roads to figure this Love thing out.

When you left me before tears became streams

And life was missing my lady.

I thought of you every day and since

That time as the chariots turned into cars.

Our souls have been traveling with time.

Leaving bodies and moving to another one

Hoping to find you again.

Our eyes have met one time before

Long ago in that special place.

Robbed

Why Was I Robbed

Of My Home Land?

Taken On A Journey

To The Unknown

Who Shall I Pray To

For Hope And Gains Or

Should I Just Look Inside Of Me?

What Will It Take?

You took me back to the past
Your beauty seems to last
Just like time which goes by
My heart is pounding as I get near you
So I can give you love the kind you deserve

Chorus
What will it take to win your heart?
What will it take to gain your trust?
What will it take for us to be family?
What will it take to let love rule our life?

Is that really you woman?
You have not changed a bit
There were some good times on the yard lady
We grew up there and became men and women
Having to face our responsibility,
I would love to call you and keep in touch

Chorus
What will it take to win your heart?
What will it take to gain your trust?
What will it take for us to be family?
What will it take to let love rule our life?

Woman this is the best time I had in years
Just let your fears go and fall in love with me
I will make you happy just wait and see
It is time for us to be family
And trust each other with our love

Chorus
What will it take to win your heart?
What will it take to gain your trust?
What will it take for us to be family?
What will it take to let love rule our life?

IF You Can Hold On

Girl you know, I am just coming out of a relationship
I need love and I want to touch you
But if you are looking for someone to hold on to
Every night of the week
I might not can find the time right now

Chorus
You can be down, but don't push it
Our love will eventually come around
If you can hold on to our love
We will find a way for it to grow

I been through some hard times with that ex love of mine
My heart can share some time with you woman
But not all my time right now can't you see
But If you let me come around and see you
I will make love to you, just like you are mine

Chorus
You can be down, but don't push it
Our Love will eventually come around
If you can hold on to our love
We will find a way for it to grow

I know woman you need love everyday
And you want it right now
Let our relationship grow into love
We can be patient and caring for each other
And love will find away into our hearts

Chorus
You can be down, but don't push it
Our love will eventually come around
If you can hold on to our love
We will find a way for it to grow

Host Of Host

People say who they are why does
Everybody have to run game
Using your name in vain, just like
When it rains it pours down water on the earth
Love is a gift from you to him, And from you to her
But sometimes what we do or say
Shocks our love ones and lead them a stray

Lord God host of host
He who gives us insight
Lord God host of host
You are the light of this world

When will our people be free to love
And have a one on one relationship
With God, and their love ones
Why do we hurt the ones that are close to us?
Can you see God knows all?
That is in our hearts and souls.

Lord God host of hosts
He who gives us insight
Lord God host of host
You are the light of this world

Will Love ever reign supreme on this earth?
Or doubt take us down the road of temptation
And Lead us straight into a fire of no return
Or will our ancestors intervene and help lead us to the light?
The other side is not far away, we will see

Lord God host of host
He who gives us insight
Lord God host of host
You are the light of this world

Over Night

God said who, ever takes a wife treat her
As your equal and be sure to love her right
Even when some days you will not get along
Please hang in there and be strong
You got people around you
Hoping that your love will fall down
Because they live in a heart break town
Keep your heart and faith in God
He is the key to love and all the joy it brings

It did not happen overnight
It might take years to make it right
Because if you are husband and wife
Love will make it right

Have you ever fell on your knees
And prayed and humbled yourself?
Oh God please forgive me I love my wife
I did not mean the things I said
She is my gift God, from you to me
Who listens to me when no one else cares?
I will hold her and comfort her
As we share love each and every night

It did not happen over night
It might take years to make it right
Because if you are husband and wife
Love will make it right

Between The Lines Of Your Life

Sometimes you have to check yourself out,
Look within your heart before you make that next move.
Is love ruling your life or the things you have, become addicted to?
What is around the block, when you turn on that corner?

Chorus
Can you read between the lines of your life?
Do you think you are going to be my wife?
Can you read between the lines of your life?
Will you be able to prescribed that love is the way?

Have you check your relationship today?
Did you and your lady have a deep conversation on life?
Were the flowers fresh today, or are the dead ones still in the vase?
Have you looked between the sheets today, to see if she was under
the cover?

Chorus
Can you read between the lines of your life?
Do you think you are going to be my wife?
Can you read between the lines of your life?
Will you be able to prescribed that love is the way?

If you had love and you lost it
And you never could replace it with someone else
Will you find her and tell her, that she was the soul mate
And no one could ever give you the love she has?
How many lonely nights must I endure?
To make sure you are near my heart again, one day and many nights
I am hoping to kiss you and touch you, just like we use to.

Chorus
Can you read between the lines of your life?
Do you think you are going to be my wife?
Can you read between the lines of your life?
Will you be able to prescribed that love is the way?

We All Have To Go, There Is Nothing That Can Stop It

For Michael Jackson

No more shadow will follow you around

No more press who did not understand

And tried to keep you down

You entertained us with your heart and soul

And in return you touched the world

And men and women became human beings again

No more shadow will follow you around

But the love you gave mankind will last forever

Your kindness and giving to people in need

The world gave your art the respect it deserved

And you became one of the greatest entertainers of all time

The Ka (spirit) is endless but the flesh will perish

Love Is Not A Faucet

Why do people think they can control you?
And turn you on like a faucet
Hot one moment then cold
Are their relationships based on love?
Did God put us here to dream of life and luxury's
To ease your mind and cool your soul?

Love is not a faucet
To turn on and off at your command
Stick with a plan to
Win your woman or man

You do not have the power to
Turn me off or on
One minute you are on and then the next I am alone
Make up your mind before you start to play
Cause love is not a faucet to turn on then turn off
Just think if two people played that game
It would be turned off more than on
Who wants to live that way hot, cold, and lukewarm?

Love is not a faucet
To turn on and off at your command
Stick with a plan to
Win your woman or man

Angel Line

You know Squirrel you been all over the world

Is it now the time to sing your stories in a song?

To make it across the Angel Line

Dedication, Perseverance, Hard Work, Talent

Faith = Belief in some divine purpose behind

Your action and preparation

Grind

They got the whip on my back

This man ain't giving me know slack

I got a scanner gun and I am on the run

When I scan the barcode I get my time

20 years on the run before I can see the day

My nights were my lights

My bed ease my pain

The dreams were Incomplete, I was on the run again

My compensation for running were meager

But I enjoyed getting up in the morning

There was no place I would rather be than to grind

One Kiss Away

When we were together all those years
We never learned to know each other
You told me you love me
And all the changes we have been through
I was there for you and then one day
You walked away and our love was lost

Do you know love is just around the corner?
It is one kiss away from our hearts
Do you know love is just around the corner?
Because we broke up, we can make up too

You gave me a lifetime guarantee
But no warranty came with the relationship
That lasted then it was gone
You had time for yourself, but did you ever
Come by to give her flowers, or just
Tell her how good she looked that day

Do you know love is just around the corner?
It is one kiss away from our hearts
Do you know love is just around the corner?
Because we broke up, we can make up too

Did you ever go by the house?
And knock on the door and ask her
Can I come home I really do miss you?
I am tired of being alone baby
Why did we have to fuss and cuss?
It only made us grow far apart
I need to love you only

Did you know love is just around the corner?
It is one kiss away from our hearts
Do you know love is just around the corner?
Because we broke up, we can make up too

If We Could Love

We long for love to be happy
And we dream the night away in our fantasy
And we hope tomorrow brings a new day
And we struggle every day to keep our life in order
If we could love for just one day
If we could sing a song for peace
If we could stop the world from turning
If we could let human beings be free
We look into the eyes of hope and desires
And we wonder if our world is really changing
And we search for mysteries of life untold
And we put our souls into the hands of our holy men
If we could love for just one day
If we could sing a song for peace
If we could stop the world from turning
If we could let human beings be free
We defeated our slave master with peace and love
And we reached the highest seat in our land
And we believe change is going to come
And we know God is near our heart walking us through
If we could love for just one day
If we could sing a song for peace
If we could stop the world from turning
If we could let human beings be free
If the day could see tomorrow and time
Could stop for a moment, would love reveal
Itself to those whose hearts are not hardened
By life and the journeys they have been on
Could man know peace and tranquility
Without producing weapons of mass destruction?
Could life take on a new meaning and bring us
Into the abundance of joy, If the day could see tomorrow
Will our hearts become one?

Forever Believing In Achieving

Face your fears

Reverse you Fears

To be Afraid is a hindrance

Your name will take on

The energy of your will

You Take on the energy of the name

 Passion

Dedicated to my friend

Alicia Cherry

Shahar = Sunrise, Dawn in Hebrew

I woke up in the morning, near you

And my life was complete

Love was my shadow to see you again

Another day so I can pray

Hopefully mankind will be able

To see the vision, to change his way

Maybe because I am a good man

I can practice what I believe

The star that shined bright in the night sky

Is it a sign of our times

To open up our eyes to see

I need you by my side to encourage me

So I can have hope to fulfill my destiny

The one God bestowed on me

I Can't Sleep At Night

There is no more game left in me
Only loving you would seem just right
You come into my life at a moment
When love seem to be out of sight
You might be my wife a friend of mine for life

I Can't Sleep at night cause
I am thinking about holding on to you tight

I just want to love you woman
The way God meant it to be
Will you be the one tonight?
And the rest of my days on this earth
There is no way in this world
That our love will not grow
We have to take our time and let this affair be right

I Can't Sleep at night cause
I am thinking about holding on to you tight

God's light led you to me on a night
Full of miracles and love delights
I will not be denied true love, it resides
Inside both of our hearts, the true meaning
Of our purpose the reason why we met

I Can't Sleep at night cause
I am thinking about holding on to you tight

I hoped and pray that love will reign supreme
I can never let you go away
This love was meant to stay
I Can't Sleep at night cause
I am thinking about holding on to you tight

The Angels Of God

Some of us have Danced in the drunken dens of
Modern day society and polluted our minds with, Heroin
Jim Beam, pharmaceuticals, Cocaine, and sipped on Bloody Mary's
My God has created everything and given us
The capacity to change mankind, it is about time for mankind
To start respecting everybody's faith in God

The Angels of God have followed me
And they led me to the Red Sea
The Angels of God have followed me
And they led me to you can't you see

I prayed on the blessed mountain
That peace would come on earth
And I threw stones at the devil to get him off my back
Our God will not forsake us he is
The hidden one in everybody's soul
Let us wake up and see the light of love
It is right there in front of all of us

The Angels of God have followed me
And they led me to the Red Sea
The Angels of God have followed me
And they led me to you can't you see

I been on journeys that I never should have taken
But God is the master of our destiny
He is the care taker of life
God can bring you back from the fire of destruction
And give you instruction on how to
Be a better man in his all seeing eye

The Angels of God have followed me
And they led me to the Red Sea
The Angels of God have followed me
And they led me to you can't you see

I Am The One

We gonna move you, out of your seats
You are gonna remember us just feel the beat
We come to sing to you
Our voices are full of Soul

Chorus
If you got love in your heart
I am the one that can feel the part

We are sisters from a family of love
God bless us from above to be with you
Let our love for the music
Bring us closer to our world

Chorus
If you got love in your heart
I am the one that can feel the part

We have hope and dreams to be singing stars
Playing our music in arenas and at your local bar
I hope you are up dancing
Showing us love on our second time around

Chorus
If you got love in your heart
I am the one that can feel the part

This song is for Ejypt = Joy, Kat,Temell, and Sophia

Your Work

Find your work and you will sustain your life goals

Find your gift and do not worry about your job

When once you confess in Allah, God, Amon, Yah-Weh,

Jehovah, Buddha, Jesus, you will be tested by the bad (satan)

And it is up to you to with stand

And stay on the right path

And do not succumb to the kingdom of evil

Are you doing the right thing for the wrong reason

And no matter what season it is,

Goodness is that which is on your heart

Am I Your Man?

Do you miss me?
Do you Love me?
Do you miss me?
Am I your man?

We broke up and I am all choked up
I don't know what to say woman
To get us back together
Can I come over tonight and talk to you?
We will go on a walk and cool this thing off

Do you miss me?
Do you love me?
Do you miss me?
Am I your man?

I hope you are not seeing anybody else
Because nobody but me
Will be able to love you right
You know our connection is tight
And the love we share is real woman
I can deal with you all the time

Do you miss me?
Do you love me?
Do you miss me?
Am I your man?

A Moment

We can enjoy our moments

Then our life will be complete

And searching for that special one

Will come at the blink of our eyes

To feel love and run from it and hide your feelings

It is like seeking the material gains of our world

It molds a plastic mentality and you think you are real

But you are caught up in the secular world

And your spirituality is drained by your ambitions and drive

You look beyond love and the world becomes your loneliness

While the almighty dollar becomes your God

My Kisses

My heart beats are just for you lady
You just can't imagine how you make me feel
When our faces met face to face
I was consumed by the moment
And never will I leave your side
I do not believe in magic, but the angels
Were there blessing that moment of our embrace

Chorus
My Kisses belong to you baby
Know other woman will feel my lips again

I will pray and hope that our love will last
Because without you by my side
This life of mine would just have been a lie
To finally meet your soul mate
The one your inner God had made just for you

Chorus
My Kisses belong to you baby
Know other woman will feel my lips again

The hidden one inside of me
Guided me to you
It was not luck but faith that brought us together
When love is in the air, there are two heart beats
That really matter yours and mine

Chorus
My Kisses belong to you baby
Know other woman will feel my lips again

Hawa = Wish

I wish the Oromo were free in Ethiopia

They represent the Ancient Kemetic Cushite community

Of Africa.

Their customs date back to the beginning of time.

Oh God why cant there be peace in Ethiopia?

Wars and Rumors of wars, famines and injustice

To a people who has not done any wrong.

They want peace, love, truth, and wisdom.

That is their way of life.

Let the Oromo vote and give

Them respect in their land.

Let their political prisoners be free

Free the Oromo, for they are a loving people!

They only want, what is right for their

Brother and Sister.

Hawa, Hawa, Hawa, Hawa, Hawa

I wish for peace, I wish for love,

I wish for truth, I wish for wisdom!

The Key To Your Heart

Hello Baby, your look, smile and mind got me going
And I want the whole world to know
I love you and care for you woman
My nights and days will not be right
If I can't touch you and see you and hear your voice

Chorus
Can I get the key to your heart?
Will you let me unlock your love?

Hello Baby, your love is the one I dream about
And having you loving me
Our life will be filled with ecstasy
You are my inspiration my life long sensation
My reality is other people dreams, my desire is loving
You always

Chorus
Can I get the key to your heart?
Will you let me unlock your love?

Teka

Your beauty is timeless

Like a star lit night off a country road

Looking up in the night sky

A, African American Queen

Who has love for life

That will keep her spirit

Going for an infinite amount of time

You are a blessing in disguise

An Angel full of love

To help guide me to my destiny

We Can't Hide It or Deny It

I talk to a woman she was so sweet and kind
She made me think of love again
And with all the pain, my life has put me through
Woman I choose you to be my woman
To spend the rest of my life loving you
If you only you knew, that we were supposed to meet
And our encounter was heavenly
A divine meeting of the minds

We can't hide it or deny it
Follow what your mind says is right

We meet again baby and love is on my mind
I can never let you go away
This love was meant to stay right here
I knew we would meet again
Because God would not deny me of true love again
If you are my woman, love will reign supreme
In time the true meaning of our love
The reason why we met will be revealed

We can't hide it or deny it
Follow what your mind says is right

You Got Me Hustling

You got me hustling for you love, just you and me!
You got me hustling for your love, just you and me!

Slinging rock cocaine from sun up to sun down
How many families have I broken up?
And how many kids have lost their lives
On the streets of this hustler paradise?
Is my conscious finally getting to me?
Should I have love for my human family
Or will this gangster life take me to prison
Or to my death?

You got me hustling for your love, just you and me!
You got me hustling for your love, just you and me!

I can't get any sleep at night you see
Wondering if someone is going to rob me
With my 9 millimeter on one side
And my lady on the other side
I been thinking, there is got to be another way
To make this money and get my life on the right side
What kind of example am I making for my sons?
I surely do not want them in this game

You got me hustling for your love, just you and me!
You got me hustling for your love, just you and me!

Cocaine has been my way of life for so long
I know I can give it up and become a born again citizen
Open up a business and get into the legitimate game
Sometimes money takes us to our dark side
And we never find a way back to the light
The streets can break you down, take your soul
And leave you a hollow man

You got me hustling for your love, just you and me!
You got me hustling for your love, just you and me!

Nannyism

Don't fool around with trash

It will get in your eyes

You might think the grass is greener

On the other side but it is probably not

Nannyism

Aunt Haggard's children are still killing

Each other

And they will continue doing it

You can not change their way and the world

Nannyism

You can lead a horse to the well

But you can't make him drink the water

Get your education you are

Going to be paying a dollar for bread

And a dollar for a gallon of gas

Food For Thought

If we are to free ourselves from ourselves.

Why does our world lack compassion

And love for our fellow Human Beings

Regardless of their race, religion, and

The region of the world they were born in?

Look inside your heart mankind

And let us find a way.

Al Hajji Robert J. Rowland

Look

The eyes that smile are full of joy and love.

They can pull you in and hope will begin

To everlasting relationship with love with no limits.

The eyes they tell a story of how long we have walked on earth

They are also wide and open when a new birth looks on

To their new world

The eyes reveal mystery of places and time

Seen and unseen, archaeological finds, links to DNA

Of educated black men Ruling the earth with peace.

No weapons of mass destruction only peace, love and wisdom.

Look and you will see, look over, look into, look out.

Look to your God inside of you!

Food For Thought

Time is the instrument that will bring

All things together that are meant to be

The indoctrination of the fabrication of the Ancient

Indigenous Black Kemetic African (Egyptian) on

His Continent is antiquated and is in need of updating

To include the real contributions that have been made

By their cultural to our modern world

In the school rooms around the world

Al Hajji Robert J. Rowland

Food For Thought

If the education system continued to promote

European history. And keep African (Kemetic), Arab

Hispanic, East Indian, North American Indian

(Mayan & Incan) and Asian, history out of the class rooms

The dropout rate in the inner cities and rural areas of America

Will continue to be astronomical. Our children are the key to

Reshaping our world. Let know child be left behind

By making all races inclusive in our educational system.

The truth will set us free, no race is superior to another!

Al Hajji Robert J. Rowland

Food For Thought

What path is mankind on?

What road will you choose?

Are you on the inside looking out at everybody?

Judging their ways, knowing you are right

But do you have a clue or a taste of knowledge

That will get you through the streets of life

And take you beyond?

Al Hajji Robert J. Rowland

All I Care

I think about you all the time, you
Are standing there right in front of my eyes
Love was so close I could taste it
You are the one that exceptional one
That woman that most men do not want to approach

All I care about is dreaming
All I care about is singing
All I want from you is that you love me
All I want from you is that you please me

They know they have to be for real
No one night, stand with you woman
It has to be a commitment for the rest of your life
With a ring and a wedding ceremony
A house by the sea for the two of us

All I care about is dreaming
All I care about is singing
All I want from you is that you love me
All I want from you is that you please me

Miss You

You look like my queen

So regal and supreme

You are so beautiful you drew me in

Wanting to get close to you

In your presence I forget about the despair

Of the world and the children starving

Because of mankind's greed and lust for money

Could I be the man for you

And we learn to love each other?

It might take a life time and a whole lot of compromises

Will you be willing to pray to God (Amun)

To protect our souls from the evil, that is

Embedded in our society?

In your dreams do you believe love is the cure

To solve humanities racial problems?

My Queen are you willing to take a chance on love

And cross the line of cultural differences

Language barriers, different religious beliefs

All in the name of love?

The Hooks

You got that trunk in the bunk

We gonna keep the funk on the run

I hope you are having some fun

Because love will keep you funking

I remember the first time I met you

But I can't remember the last time I saw you

Don't Look for trouble, where it aint

If you can find love just trust it

The Mountain Top

Just when you think that life has passed you by
There was no hope, you did not think about tomorrow
Then one of your best friends dies and they go to the other side
The light within started to shine and you could see again

I just want to sing this song, like God meant it to be
I just want to live my life and make my dreams come true
I just want to say to myself that I gave it my all that 100%
I just want to reach the mountain top and never forget how I got
there

I got a phone call from a special lady friend
We had kept each other on hold waiting to see if it was meant to be
Everybody needs a hug and some companionship you see
I got enough baby mamas and I surely don't need no baby drama

I just want to sing this song, like God meant it to be
I just want to live my life and make my dreams come true
I just want to say to myself that I gave it my all that 100%
I just want to reach the mountain top and never forget how I got
there

I started mapping out a future and dreams became reality
Then I took my car keys and began to drive up town
When I got to my destination there was no stopping me now
I had arrived at the top the show was about to begin

For every will God will find a way for you to shine

I just want to sing this song, like God meant it to be
I just want to live my life and make my dreams come true
I just want to say to myself that I gave it my all that 100%
I just want to reach the mountain top and never forget how I got
there

Inside Or Outside

We can talk the night away

We can sing until the morning comes

We can learn to love again

From the mistakes we made in our past

Love was meant for two

And only the fools will be left alone

When I look into your eyes

I see a future near your side

Will you let me in your heart my friend?

Or will I be standing on the outside wondering?

Food For Thought

I am tired of Christianity, Buddhism, Hinduism,

Judaism and Islam in their slavery and colonialist form.

No religions are above God and no race of people is

Superior to another, we are Human beings

That is our God given commonality.

Al Hajji Robert J Rowland

Nannyism

Loose lips sink ships

My Brother

To my young brother the man, when dad left us I thought

Nanny would be alone

But to my surprise my brother was at the house every day.

If she needed transportation or a ride he was there to make

sure she got to her destination.

I like to thank my young brother Damon Rowland for

watching over our mother

Where ever I might be when you read this poem.

I love my family and may our kids, keep our family strong.

And may we forgive those who done us wrong.

Where Have You Been

I been lost between Africa and America
Searching for my freedom and my home
Sold into slavery working for free to survive
Did not have any love for anybody
Then I remember my spirituality, My God
My dignity, my ancestors and their contributions
To the human family
Why do I have to steal and rob my brother's?
And join a gang and take a life in your Initiation.
Is not life worth more, than to sell your soul
To some evil plan
In the past I been ban from living the American way
Just because of my color.
Now I deny myself an education, a dream and hope
Where have you been my people!

We are in the 21st Century, release the shackles
That bound your mind
We are above the despair of the Hoods
And can achieve anything we put our minds too
Turn the alarm clock on, get up and find away

New Journey

Time stood still for a moment

As I looked into your eyes

Or was it a minute, an hour, a day

A month, an year , a lifetime

A Kemetic Queen returns to earth again

To relived another cycle of life

To bring us joy and happiness

To heal the sick and uplift people

Who cross your path

May your destiny this time around

Fulfill your wildest imagination and earthly desire

The future is yours to master

May God have blessing on your new journey.

Puddle Of Tears

A puddle of tears surround me

Is God telling me to let it go?

Put it in my hands, the spirit said

Some things are just not meant to be

Our hearts are fragile and sometimes

If we allow it, they can be broken

But remember when we pick up the broken pieces

And mend them back together

That last piece, is his or hers

And that is all they deserve

We have to move on in our life

Cause surely God will lead us

On the right path of that right choice

My Father – Team Player

Every Team my father played on or coached

His teams were in shape, they were fundamentally sound

Executed their offense as well as their defense

With precision of a master crafter,

They competed and gave 100% and in the

Outcome his teams were winners on the field and in life

Now he is going to be on the best team

The team that God has designed

And everyone there is on the first team

No bench warmers, they are all starters

And each an everyone has that heavenly bliss

Something we lack on this side of God's team

May God give my family the strength to carry on

Just One

To go beyond your imagination

To reach the essence of life

God flows within you

Each and every one of us has felt the presence

The inner beauty of mankind has no limits

Only you or me can taint our souls

Love cannot be taught, bought or sold

It lies deep in our nature waiting to be awakened

By our family, our desires, and our love mates

Mankind we are free to live our life and prepare our death

The oneness of God is ever near us please do not let it go

I beg of you, mankind, there are plenty of colors

But we are just one Human Race.

In Time At The Gathering

When that day comes, that we shall meet the one

Who is responsible for us being here?

No one will be left out of the gathering

It will be a time for us to be judged

Will your heart out weigh the feather of life

At the scales of justice, you see?

Will you cross the bridge of Sirat

At the speed of light into paradise?

Did you do enough right in your time on earth?

Did you make it right with the most, high, just in time?

Did you find away, to love your wife, husband, mother,

Father, sister brothers, cousin, children and your neighbors in time?

Did your spiritual side over take Satan's way in time?

Do you think that you will ever understand in time?

Shantay

I am looking forward to holding you and kissing you again
I want to run my fingers through your hair
And touch you and caress your body, like you never had before
We were like a glove and a hand, that perfect fit

You are my lady, you are my woman
You are my friend, until the end

All the nights I lie in my bed thinking about you
I can not wait to get inside of you
It is something we both need and miss
Good love comes around maybe once in a lifetime

You are my lady, you are my woman
You are my friend, until the end

I want to make this love right, I been in to many affairs
I am so into you, if you really only knew
Just believe in me and I will believe in you
And love will succeed and all our dreams will come true
Happiness is the key just let me in and you will see

You are my lady, you are my woman
You are my friend, until the end

I will be with you, through thick and thin
Money can not buy everything and love is real
I am anticipating the next time I see you
On our island paradise, I love you with all my heart

You are my lady, you are my woman
You are my friend, until the end

Savita

How many times have I looked up to the sun

To watch it set and to watch it rise

But have you ever walked upon the sun

To look into her eyes, face to face?

To see the beauty that she possessed

Her smile so radiant, her soul so in tune

To the cosmic forces of the universe

So independent and free, she only submits

To the will of God, as the sun fades away

I hear the leaves with a push from the wind

Roll right in front of me

I hear the birds chirping a melody

And I realize that the sun has inspired again

The first 4 letters of her last name Maat= Ancient Kemitic,, Truth Justice, Peace, love wisdom and Balance.

Wangari Maathai
1940 – 2011
She came, she went, a very powerful woman with a silent voice

She stood up for justice and peace, Democracy was her hope for

Kenya

Which at the time had a repressive and autocratic ruler, that

stood

For greed and not the distribution of wealth to the people of the

land

She decided to plant trees and over 30 million were planted

Wangari Maathai, became the tree mother of Africa looking for

peace

She also was the first African female winner of the Nobel Peace

Prize in 2004

You were strong and educated and was protected by God

Your spirit will live on my sister we miss you

Your trees will grow strong and our human family lost another

good one.

What Do You Like?

Woman what is your favorite color?
Do you like the sunrise or the sun set?
Is your favorite flowers roses or carnations?
Do you like cotton or silk sheets?

Did you see me that day, the way I saw you?
Are you looking for a relationship? a one on one I hope!

Do you believe in love and your soulmate?
Do you taste like your chocolate complexion?
Are you sweeter than the taste of honey?
Do you want to be lonely tonight?

Did you see me that day, the way I saw you?
Are you looking for a relationship? a one on one I hope?

Will you share your bedroom
with this stranger just on sight?
Let me take you away to a place
Where pleasure exist almost
Close to that heavenly bliss!

Did you see me that day, the way I saw you?
Are you looking for a relationship? a one on one I hope!

One Day

I woke in time just to hear her voice.

Was it a phone call I just made?

Am I dreaming of her? Or is reality sinking in?

Will she be the one? Only time will tell as usual!

What was the reason of our brief encounter?

And now we are trying to restore passion, lust,

Arrangements and friendships.

Will love prevail or our imagination take us from reality?

Will God oversee our modern day religions?

And bring humanity close to the oneness of his true manifestations.

How did Serapis become the Soter?

Better known as Jesus Christ, the Father, the Son, and the Holy

Ghost.

Will my one God be with me in the valley of death?

As He has been with me on the mountain of my life.

Only Your Love

I was driving along on a road that night
And love hit me like cupid's arrow piercing my heart
No more games for me, only that one true love
You are so precious, amazing, desirable and loveable

Only your love, we step into each other's life
Only your love, now is the time to make it right
Only your love, we open our hearts for love
Only your love, now will God give us the gift of trust from above

I will go anywhere for you my woman
I will do anything for your love. Just take my word as my bond
Baby this is not about a con job
My heart and mind are open lady. I am able to feel love again

Only your love, we step into each other's life
Only your love, now is the time to make it right
Only your love, we open our hearts for love
Only your love, now will God give us the gift of trust from above

I won't cheat on you, woman never
I will be your man if you just let me love you
The closer I get to you, woman, the more I want you by my side
Two hearts coming together for love and a dream came true

Only your love, we, step into each other's life
Only your love, now is the time to make it right
Only your love, we open our hearts for love
Only your love, now will God give us the gift of trust from above

You Are My Angel

The first night I went to your house
I needed someone to talk to and hear me out
It was something about you, that made me want to know you
I wanted to hug you and kiss you, and make love to you like you
were my woman
But one night with you could not make either one of us happy
I need to see you every day and be by your side

You are my angel the one I can touch and hold
You are my angel the one I can tell all my secrets to
You are my angel the one God chose for me to meet
You are my angel the one I can share my life with

Only God knows what is in my heart
And woman I could never hurt you
I only want to love you and be a part of your life
The stars aligned in the right place that day
We met and our destiny is in our hands
Forever just you and me that is all my eyes can see

You are my angel the one I can touch and hold
You are my angel the one I can tell all my secrets to
You are my angel the one God chose for me to meet
You are my angel the one I can share my life with

I Didn't Do It

Why do I have to deal with your past relationship?
Didn't you take the time to let it heal
So you can learn to love again?
Or was it something I said or did?

I didn't do it. I didn't break your heart.
I didn't do it. He was an imposter playing his part.
I didn't do it. Leave your relationship in the past.
I didn't do it. Move on to the new one and make it last.

All I want to do woman is to treat you nice.
Why do I have to hear about what somebody else did?
You have to move on and enjoy your life.
How can you ever become somebody else's wife?

I didn't do it. I didn't break your heart.
I didn't do it. He was an imposter playing his part.
I didn't do it. Leave your relationship in the past.
I didn't do it. Move on to the new one and make it last.

I want to buy you diamond rings.
And take you to the classist night clubs.
We will have a house overlooking the Oakland Bay.
You will be my Queen honey every day of the year.

I didn't do it. I didn't break your heart.
I didn't do it. He was an imposter playing his part.
I didn't do it. Leave your relationship in the past.
I didn't do it. Move on to the new one and make it last.

I Am In Ecstasy Baby

Man
I want to make love to you, I got to have those lovely kisses
I need to touch you in that spot, you instructed me to touch
I want to forever be your man, for as long as I can
I love to share my secrets thoughts, with you my woman

Please keep on doing what you do
Cause I am in Ecstasy baby

Woman
Please whisper in my ear, and tell me you love me my dear
Hold me and kiss me and don't let go until I tell you so
I am your woman and I will be down with whatever pleases you
Let us keep this moment cause our love is so real

Please keep on doing what you do
Cause I am in Ecstasy baby

Both
Love can be real, if you take a chance on it
There might be some conflicts but with communication
You will be in my arms again hugging me
And making good love all through the night

Please keep on doing what you do
Cause I am in Ecstasy baby

Food For Thought

Challenge beyond the essence of life existence

What course does a man take

To get back in the race of respectability

If you are a responsible one

Is the guaranteed of money

Longevity, and love waiting at your doorstep

In your mind, is there a key to turn on the soul

Why has God been on a manipulate path for mankind in his hands

Mystery lurking within, will they come out to reveal who we really

Are

In the realization of self, you will not be control or believe in fear

Quotes For Inspiration

"If you do what you've always done, you'll get what you've always gotten."
   - Anthony Robbins

"Decisiveness is a characteristic of high-performing men and women. Almost any decision is better than no decision at all."
   - Brian Tracy

"I hated every minute of training, but I said, 'Dont quit. Suffer now and live the rest of your life as a champion.'"
   - Muhammad Ali

"By failing to prepare, you are preparing to fail."
   - Benjamin Franklin

"Each time someone stands up for an ideal, or acts to improve the lot of others, or strikes out against injustice, he sends forth a tiny ripple of hope."
   - Robert F. Kennedy

"Courage is rightly esteemed the first of human qualities... because it is the quality which guarantees all others."
   - Winston Churchill

"Accept everything about yourself - I mean everything, You are you and that is the beginning and the end - no apologies, no regrets."
   - Henry A. Kissinger

"Never be satisfied with what you achieve, because it all pales in comparison with what you are capable of doing in the future."
   - Rabbi Nochem Kaplan

"Tough times never last, but tough people do."
   - Dr. Robert Schuller

"An average person with average talent, ambition and education, can outstrip the most brilliant genius in our society, if that person has clear, focused goals."
- Brian Tracy

"If you could kick the person in the pants responsible for most of your trouble, you wouldn't sit for a month."
- Theodore Roosevelt

"Dictionary is the only place that success comes before work. Hard work is the price we must pay for success. I think you can accomplish anything if you're willing to pay the price."
- Vince Lombardi

"To be a great champion you must believe you are the best. If you're not, pretend you are."
- Muhammad Ali

"There are certain bridges that are not worth crossing, no matter what others think. Loyalty and relationships are important."
- Tony Dungy

"Men's best successes come after their disappointments."
- Henry Ward Beecher

"Believe you can and you're halfway there."
- Theodore Roosevelt

"Goals allow you to control the direction of change in your favor."
- Brian Tracy

"Most successful men have not achieved their distinction by having some new talent or opportunity presented to them. They have developed the opportunity that was at hand."
-Bruce Barton

"It is our attitude at the beginning of a difficult task which, more than anything else, will affect it's successful outcome."
- William James

"Unless you're willing to have a go, fail miserably, and have another go, success won't happen."
 - Phillip Adams

"He who is not courageous enough to take risks will accomplish nothing in life."
 - Muhammad Ali

"There's a difference between interest and commitment. When you're interested in doing something, you do it only when it's convenient. When you're committed to something, you accept no excuses; only results."
 - Kenneth Blanchard

"Being defeated is often temporary, giving up makes it permanent."
 - Marilyn Von Savant

"An idea can turn to dust or magic, depending on the talent that rubs against it."
 - Bill Bernbach

"Failures do what is tension relieving, while winners do what is goal achieving."
 - Dennis Waitley

"It's easy to have faith in yourself and have discipline when you're a winner, when you're number one. What you got to have is faith and discipline when you're not a winner."
 - Vince Lombardi

"It is noble to teach oneself, but still nobler to teach others."
 - Mark Twain

"Decisiveness is a characteristic of high-performing men and women. Almost any decision is better than no decision at all."
 - Brian Tracy

"Courtesy is as much a mark of a gentleman as courage."
- Theodore Roosevelt

"Obstacles are those frightful things you see when you take your eyes off your goal."
- Henry Ford

"Always do everything you ask of those you command."
- George S. Patton

"About morals, I know only that what is moral is what you feel good after and what is immoral is what you feel bad after."
- Ernest Hemingway

"Any man who can drive safely while kissing a pretty girl is simply not giving the kiss the attention it deserves."
- Albert Einstein

"If you only do what you know you can do- you never do very much."
- Tom Krause

"The difference between a successful person and others is not a lack of strength, not a lack of knowledge, but rather a lack of will."
- Vince Lombardi

"The difference between the possible and the impossible lies in a person's determination."
- Tommy Lasorda

"Unrest of spirit is a mark of life; one problem after another presents itself and in the solving of them we can find our greatest pleasure."
- Kal Menninger

"I've found that luck is quite predictable. If you want more luck, take more chances. Be more active. Show up more often."
- Brian Tracy

"Courage doesn't always roar. Sometimes courage is the quiet voice at the end of the day saying, 'I will try again tomorrow.'"
- Mary Anne Radmacher

"The price of hating other human beings is loving oneself less."
- Eldridge Cleaver

"It is better to run today than to wait until tomorrow"
-   Al Hajji Robert J Rowland

"Most people seek after what they do not possess and are thus enslaved by the very things they want to acquire."
- Anwar El-Sadat

"If you believe in yourself and have dedication and pride - and never quit, you'll be a winner. The price of victory is high but so are the rewards."
- Paul Bryant

"The greatest mistake you can make in life is to continually be afraid you will make one."
- Elbert Hubbard

"If you don't design your own life plan, chances are you'll fall into someone else's plan. And guess what they have planned for you? Not much."
- Jim Rohn

"Far better is it to dare mighty things, to win glorious triumphs, even though checkered by failure... than to rank with those poor spirits who neither enjoy nor suffer much, because they live in a gray twilight that knows not victory nor defeat."
- Theodore Roosevelt

"If you'll not settle for anything less than your best, you will be amazed at what you can accomplish in your lives."
- Vince Lombardi

A vote is like a rifle; its usefulness depends upon the character of the user."
- Theodore Roosevelt

"Freedom consists not in doing what we like, but in having the right to do what we ought."
- Pope John Paul II

"Hard work spotlights the character of people: some turn up their sleeves, some turn up their noses, and some don't turn up at all."
- Sam Ewing

"A wise man is superior to any insults which can be put upon him, and the best reply to unseemly behavior is patience and moderation."
- Moliere

Happiness is not something you postpone for the future; it is something you design for the present."
- Jim Rohn

"If you can dream it, you can do it."
- Walt Disney

"Defeat is not the worst of failures. Not to have tried is the true failure."
- George Edward Woodberry

"Being powerful is like being a lady. If you have to tell people you are, you aren't."
- Margaret Thatcher

"A true friend never gets in your way unless you happen to be going down."
- Arnold H. Glasow

"Dictionary is the only place that success comes before work. Hard work is the price we must pay for success. I think you can accomplish anything if you're willing to pay the price."
- Vince Lombardi

"Always bear in mind that your own resolution to succeed is more important than any other." "Imagination will often carry us to worlds that never were. But without it we go nowhere."
- Carl Sagan

"Every year of my life I grow more convinced that it is wisest and best to fix our attention on the beautiful and the good, and dwell as little as possible on the evil and the false."
- Richard Cecil

"What lies behind us and what lies before us are tiny matters compared to what lies within us."
- Ralph Waldo Emerson

"A kiss is a lovely trick designed by nature to stop speech when words become superfluous."
- Ingrid Bergman

"A mistake is always forgivable, rarely excusable and always unacceptable."
- Robert Fripp

"Remember, a real decision is measured by the fact that you've taken new action. If there's no action, you haven't truly decided."
- Tony Robbins

"It is the mark of an educated mind to be able to entertain a thought without accepting it."
- Aristotle

"People with clear, written goals, accomplish far more in a shorter period of time than people without them could ever imagine."
- Brian Tracy

"A woman has to be intelligent, have charm, a sense of humor, and be kind. It's the same qualities I require from a man."
- Catherine Deneuve

"Perseverance is not a long race; it is many short races one after the other."
- Walter Elliot

"Human beings, who are almost unique in having the ability to learn from the experience of others, are also remarkable for their apparent disinclination to do so."
- Douglas Adams

"Pain prompts us to change behavior that is destructive to ourselves or to others. Pain can be a highly effective instructor."
- Tony Dungy

"Never tell people how to do things. Tell them what to do and they will surprise you with their ingenuity."
- George S. Patton

"Each generation goes further than the generation preceding it because it stands on the shoulders of that generation. You will have opportunities beyond anything we've ever known."
- Ronald Reagan

"Setting goals is the first step in turning the invisible into the visible."
- Tony Robbins

"He who has health, has hope; and he who has hope, has everything."
- Thomas Carlyle

"I don't believe you have to be better than everybody else. I believe you have to be better than you ever thought you could be."
- Ken Venturi

"Chains of habit are too light to be felt until they are too heavy to be broken."
- Warren Buffett

"There isn't a person anywhere who isn't capable of doing more than he thinks he can."
   - Henry Ford

"A house is not a home unless it contains food and fire for the mind as well as the body."
   - Benjamin Franklin

"Friendship with ones self is all important, because without it one cannot be friends with anyone else in the world."
   - Eleanor Roosevelt

"A vigorous five-mile walk will do more good for an unhappy but otherwise healthy adult than all the medicine and psychology in the world."
   - Paul Dudley White

"All difficult things have their origin in that which is easy, and great things in that which is small."
   - Lao Tzu
"Freedom consists not in doing what we like, but in having the right to do what we ought."
   - Pope John Paul II

"Far and away the best prize that life has to offer is the chance to work hard at work worth doing."
   - Theodore Roosevelt

"Be miserable. Or motivate yourself. Whatever has to be done, it's always your choice."
   - Wayne Dyer

"Keeping ridiculous hours doesn't mean you'll be successful."
   - Tony Dungy

"If you want to win, do the ordinary things better than anyone else does - day in and day out."
   - Chuck Noll

"Age is an issue of mind over matter. If you don't mind, it doesn't matter."
- Mark Twain

"The thing always happens that you really believe in; and the belief in a thing makes it happen."
- Frank Loyd Wright

"As you walk down the fairway of life you must smell the roses, for you only get to play one round."
- Ben Hogan

"Anger is a killing thing: it kills the man who angers, for each rage leaves him less than he had been before - it takes something from him."
- Louis L'Amour

"I honestly think it is better to be a failure at something you love than to be a success at something you hate."
- George Burns

"Adopt the pace of nature: her secret is patience."
- Ralph Waldo Emerson

"A man who trusts nobody is apt to be the kind of man nobody trusts."
- Harold MacMillan

"Big jobs usually go to the men who prove their ability to outgrow small ones."
- Theodore Roosevelt

"There is only one real sin, and that is to persuade oneself that the second-best is anything but the second-best."
- Doris Lessing

"The greatest results in life are usually attained by simple means and the exercise of ordinary qualities. These may for the most part be summed in these two: common-sense and perseverance."
   - Owen Feltham

"If your actions inspire others to dream more, learn more, do more and become more, you are a leader."
   - John Quincy Adams

"The way you think, the way you behave, the way you eat, can influence your life by 30 to 50 years."
   - Deepak Chopra

"The friend in my adversity I shall always cherish most. I can better trust those who helped to relieve the gloom of my dark hours than those who are so ready to enjoy with me the sunshine of my prosperity."
   - Ulysses Grant

"Failure is not fatal, but failure to change might be."
   - John Wooden

"A real decision is measured by the fact that you've taken a new action. If there's no action, you haven't truly decided."
   - Tony Robbins

"As a cure for worrying, work is better than whiskey."
   - Ralph Waldo Emerson

"An idealist is a person who helps other people to be prosperous."
   - Henry Ford

"I am the astronaut of boxing. Joe Louis and Dempsey were just jet pilots. I'm in a world of my own."
   - Muhammad Ali

"This is no time for ease and comfort. It is time to dare and endure."
   - Winston Churchill

"People who work together will win, whether it be against complex football defenses, or the problems of modern society."
- Vince Lombardi

"Being the richest man in the cemetery doesn't matter to me. Going to bed at night saying we've done something wonderful, that's what matters to me."
- Steve Jobs

"If everyone is thinking alike, then somebody isn't thinking."
- George S. Patton

"I hope I shall possess firmness and virtue enough to maintain what I consider the most enviable of all titles, the character of an honest man."
- George Washington

"Successful people are always looking for opportunities to help others. Unsuccessful people are always asking, 'What's in it for me?'"
- Brian Tracy

"A rock pile ceases to be a rock pile the moment a single man contemplates it, bearing within him the image of a cathedral."
- Antoine de Saint-Exupery

"One person with a belief is equal to a force of ninety-nine who have only interests."
- Peter Marshall

"Humility must always be the portion of any man who receives acclaim earned in the blood of his followers and the sacrifices of his friends."
- Dwight D. Eisenhower

"Do not overrate what you have received, nor envy others. He who envies others does not obtain peace of mind."
- Buddha

"Christmas renews our youth by stirring our wonder. The capacity for wonder has been called our most pregnant human faculty, for in it are born our art, our science, our religion."
   - Ralph W. Sockman

"Never be haughty to the humble or humble to the haughty."
   - Jefferson Davis

"Our achievements of today are but the sum total of our thoughts of yesterday. You are today where the thoughts of yesterday have brought you and you will be tomorrow where the thoughts of today take you."
   - Blaise Pascal

"Always do sober what you said you'd do drunk. That will teach you to keep your mouth shut."
   - Ernest Hemingway

"Any intelligent fool can make things bigger and more complex... It takes a touch of genius - and a lot of courage to move in the opposite direction."
   - Albert Einstein

"Freedom is never more than one generation away from extinction. We didn't pass it to our children in the bloodstream. It must be fought for, protected, and handed on for them to do the same."
   - Ronald Reagan

"If we do not discipline ourselves the world will do it for us."
   - William Feather

"Pressure is a word that is misused in our vocabulary. When you start thinking of pressure, it's because you've started to think of failure."
   - Tommy Lasorda

"All men dream, but not equally. Those who dream by night in the dusty recesses of their minds, wake in the day to find that it was vanity: but the dreamers of the day are dangerous men, for they may act on their dreams with open eyes, to make them possible."
 - T. E. Lawrence

"Failure is simply the opportunity to begin again, this time more intelligently."
 - Henry Ford

"If you don't like something, change it. If you can't change it, change your attitude."
 - Maya Angelou

A man is not old until regrets take the place of dreams."
 - John Barrymore

"A man who dares to waste one hour of time has not discovered the value of life."
 - Charles Darwin

"He that cannot forgive others breaks the bridge over which he must pass himself; for every man has need to be forgiven."
 - Thomas Fuller

"I don't measure a man's success by how high he climbs but how high he bounces when he hits bottom."
 - George S. Patton

"A small body of determined spirits fired by an unquenchable faith in their mission can alter the course of history."
 - Mohandas Gandhi

"Obstacles don't have to stop you. If you run into a wall, don't turn around and give up. Figure out how to climb it, go through it, or work around it."
 - Michael Jordan

"An education isn't how much you have committed to memory, or even how much you know. It's being able to differentiate between what you know and what you don't."
- Anatole France

"Do you know the difference between education and experience? Education is when you read the fine print; experience is what you get when you don't."
- Pete Seeger

"I still find each day too short for all the thoughts I want to think, all the walks I want to take, all the books I want to read, and all the friends I want to see."
- John Burroughs

"I learned that courage was not the absence of fear, but the triumph over it. The brave man is not he who does not feel afraid, but he who conquers that fear."
- Nelson Mandela

"Everyone who's ever taken a shower has an idea. It's the person who gets out of the shower, dries off and does something about it who makes a difference."
- Nolan Bushnell

"Those people who develop the ability to continuously acquire new and better forms of knowledge that they can apply to their work and to their lives will be the movers and shakers in our society for the indefinite future."
- Brian Tracy

"He who has never learned to obey cannot be a good commander."
- Aristotle

"Do you want to know who you are? Don't ask. Act! Action will delineate and define you."
- Thomas Jefferson

"Defeat is not the worst of failures. Not to have tried is the true failure."
- George Edward Woodberry

"All changes, even the most longed for, have their melancholy; for what we leave behind us is a part of ourselves; we must die to one life before we can enter another."
- Anatole France

"It's easy to have faith in yourself and have discipline when you're a winner, when you're number one. What you got to have is faith and discipline when you're not a winner."
- Vince Lombardi

"When you reach the end of your rope, tie a knot in it and hang on."
- Thomas Jefferson

"Goals are the fuel in the furnace of achievement."
- Brian Tracy

"Management is doing things right; leadership is doing the right things."
- Peter Drucker

"The ultimate measure of a man is not where he stands in moments of comfort, but where he stands at times of challenge and controversy."
- Martin Luther King, Jr.

"I saw the angel in the marble and carved until I set him free."
- Michelangelo

"Courage is what it takes to stand up and speak; courage is also what it takes to sit down and listen."
- Winston Churchill

"Nobody cares how much you know, until they know how much you care."
- Theodore Roosevelt

"Be careful the environment you choose for it will shape you; be careful the friends you choose for you will become like them."
- W. Clement Stone

"Happiness is not something you postpone for the future; it is something you design for the present."
- Jim Rohn

"Setting goals is the first step in turning the invisible into the visible."
- Tony Robbins

"Perseverance is not a long race; it is many short races one after the other."
- Walter Elliot

"The more you seek security, the less of it you have. But the more you seek opportunity, the more likely it is that you will achieve the security that you desire."
- Brian Tracy

"If you don't design your own life plan, chances are you'll fall into someone else's plan. And guess what they have planned for you? Not much."
- Jim Rohn

"I fear not the man who has practiced 10,000 kicks once, but I fear the man who has practiced one kick 10,000 times."
- Bruce Lee

"Don't judge each day by the harvest you reap but by the seeds that you plant."
- Robert Louis Stevenson

"A person without a sense of humor is like a wagon without springs. It's jolted by every pebble on the road."
- Henry Ward Beecher

"Criticism may not be agreeable, but it is necessary. It fulfils the same function as pain in the human body. It calls attention to an unhealthy state of things."
- Winston Churchill

"Many of the things you can count, don't count. Many of the things you can't count, really count."
- Albert Einstein

" If we love our country, we should also love our countrymen."
- Ronald Reagan

"Just as your car runs more smoothly and requires less energy to go faster and farther when the wheels are in perfect alignment, you perform better when your thoughts, feelings, emotions, goals, and values are in balance."
- Brian Tracy

"A real decision is measured by the fact that you've taken a new action. If there's no action, you haven't truly decided."
- Anthony Robbins

"A creative man is motivated by the desire to achieve, not by the desire to beat others."
- Ayn Rand

"Don't ask what the world needs. Ask what makes you come alive, and go do it. Because what the world needs is people who have come alive."
- Howard Thurman

"It is amazing what you can accomplish if you do not care who gets the credit."
- Harry Truman

"When solving problems, dig at the roots instead of just hacking at the leaves."
- Anthony J. D'Angelo

"Pain is inevitable, but misery is optional. We cannot avoid pain, but we can avoid joy."
- Tim Hansel

"The measure of who we are is what we do with what we have."
- Vince Lombardi

"What is not started today is never finished tomorrow."
- Johann Wolfgang von Goethe

"Effective leadership is not about making speeches or being liked; leadership is defined by results not attributes."
- Peter Drucker

"The price of success is hard work, dedication to the job at hand, and the determination that whether we win or lose, we have applied the best of ourselves to the task at hand."
- Vince Lombardi

"Build me a son, O Lord, who will be strong enough to know when he is weak, and brave enough to face himself when he is afraid, one who will be proud and unbending in honest defeat, and humble and gentle in victory."
- Douglas MacArthur

"The true measure of an individual is how he treats a person who can do him absolutely no good."
- Ann Landers

" The only people with whom you should try to get even are those who have helped you."
- John E. Southard

The only people with whom you should try to get even are those who have helped you."
    - John E. Southard

"Act as if what you do makes a difference. It does."
    - William James

"There's a beauty to wisdom and experience that cannot be faked. It's impossible to be mature without having lived."
    - Amy Grant

"Don't wait around for other people to be happy for you. Any happiness you get you've got to make yourself."
    - Alice Walker

"If you want to succeed you should strike out on new paths, rather than travel the worn paths of accepted success."
    - John D. Rockefeller

"The essential elements of giving are power and love - activity and affection - and the consciousness of the race testifies that in the high and appropriate exercise of these is a blessedness greater than any other."
    - Mark Hopkins

"America was not built on fear. America was built on courage, on imagination and an unbeatable determination to do the job at hand."
    - Harry S. Truman

"Setting goals is the first step in turning the invisible into the visible."
    - Tony Robbins

"I play to win, whether during practice or a real game. And I will not let anything get in the way of me and my competitive enthusiasm to win."
    - Michael Jordan

"Forgiveness is the economy of the heart... forgiveness saves the expense of anger, the cost of hatred, the waste of spirits."
- Hannah More

"So many of our dreams at first seem impossible, then they seem improbable, and then, when we summon the will, they soon become inevitable."
- Christopher Reeve

"Learning is not attained by chance, it must be sought for with ardor and diligence."
- Abigail Adams

"Everything that goes up must come down. But there comes a time when not everything that's down can come up."
- George Burns

"Every tomorrow has two handles. We can take hold of it with the handle of anxiety or the handle of faith."
- Henry Ward Beecher

"History, despite its wrenching pain, cannot be unlived, but if faced with courage, need not be lived again."
- Maya Angelou

"Remain calm, serene, always in command of yourself. You will then find out how easy it is to get along."
- Paramahansa Yogananda

"A round man cannot be expected to fit in a square hole right away. He must have time to modify his shape."
- Mark Twain

"In essence, if we want to direct our lives, we must take control of our consistent actions. It's not what we do once in a while that shapes our lives, but what we do consistently."
- Tony Robbins

"Criticism may not be agreeable, but it is necessary. It fulfils the same function as pain in the human body. It calls attention to an unhealthy state of things."
- Winston Churchill

"If I were given the opportunity to present a gift to the next generation, it would be the ability for each individual to learn to laugh at himself."
- Charles M. Shultz

"Anyone who has never made a mistake has never tried anything new."
- Albert Einstein

"Genuine forgiveness does not deny anger but faces it head-on."
- Alice Duer Miller

"If you don't have time to do it right, when will you have time to do it over?"
- John Wooden

"How pleasant it is for a father to sit at his child's board. It is like an aged man reclining under the shadow of an oak which he has planted."
- Voltaire

"All, everything that I understand, I understand only because I love."
- Leo Tolstoy

"It's not the events of our lives that shape us, but our beliefs as to what those events mean."
- Tony Robbins

"An ounce of action is worth a ton of theory."
- Ralph Waldo Emerson

"A diplomat is a man who always remembers a woman's birthday but never remembers her age."
- Robert Frost

"Courage is not simply one of the virtues, but the form of every virtue at the testing point."
   - C.S. Lewis

"A person who never made a mistake never tried anything new."
   - Albert Einstein

"If you look for truth, you may find comfort in the end; if you look for comfort you will not get either comfort or truth only soft soap and wishful thinking to begin, and in the end, despair."
   - C. S. Lewis

There is only one word you need to learn and activate to become successful, and that word is 'DO' Every time you are tempted to react in the same old way, ask if you want to be a prisoner of the past or a pioneer of the future.
   -Deepak Chopra

"A person who won't read has no advantage over one who can't read."
   - Mark Twain

Look at everything as though you were seeing it either for the first or last time. Then your time on earth will be filled with glory.
   -Betty Smith

People often say that motivation doesn't last. Well, neither does bathing - that's why we recommend it daily.
   -Zig Zaglar

"Opportunity is missed by most people because it is dressed in overalls and looks like work."
   - Thomas A. Edison

"All difficult things have their origin in that which is easy, and great things in that which is small."
   - Lao Tzu

The reason people find it so hard to be happy is that they always see the past better than it was, the present worse than it is, and the future less resolved than it will be.
    -Marcel Pagnol

Being happy doesn't mean that everything is perfect. It means that you've decided to look beyond the imperfections.
    -Unknown

The pessimist sees difficulty in every opportunity. The optimist sees the opportunity in every difficulty.
    -Winston Churchill

Dreams are renewable. No matter what our age or condition, there are still untapped possibilities within us and new beauty waiting to be born.
    -Dale E. Turner

 The trouble with not having a goal is that you can spend your life running up and down the field and never score.
    -Bill Copeland

"Associate with men of good quality if you esteem your own reputation; for it is better to be alone than in bad company."
    - George Washington

"Love of beauty is taste. The creation of beauty is art."
    - Ralph Waldo Emerson

"It is my feeling that Time ripens all things; with Time all things are revealed; Time is the father of truth."
    - Francois Rabelais

Compromise is based on give and take, but there can be no give and take on fundamentals. Any compromise on mere fundamentals is a surrender. For it is all give and no take."
    - Mahatma Gandhi

"Most of the important things in the world have been accomplished by people who have kept on trying when there seemed to be no hope at all."
- Dale Carnegie

"Never trust anyone who wants what you've got. Friend or no, envy is an overwhelming emotion."
- Eubie Blake

"A mind that is stretched by a new experience can never go back to its old dimensions."
- Oliver Wendell Holmes, Jr.

"Change means that what was before wasn't perfect. People want things to be better."
- Esther Dyson

"A woodland in full color is awesome as a forest fire, in magnitude at least, but a single tree is like a dancing tongue of flame to warm the heart."
- Hal Borland

"Perseverance is not a long race; it is many short races one after the other."
- Walter Elliot

"All men dream, but not equally. Those who dream by night in the dusty recesses of their minds, wake in the day to find that it was vanity: but the dreamers of the day are dangerous men, for they may act on their dreams with open eyes, to make them possible."
- T. E. Lawrence

"Some of us will do our jobs well and some will not, but we will be judged by only one thing - the result."
- Vince Lombardi

"A teacher affects eternity; he can never tell where his influence stops."
- Henry Adams

"Your most dangerous competitors are those that are most like you."
- Bruce Henderson

"Exercise to stimulate, not to annihilate. The world wasn't formed in a day, and neither were we. Set small goals and build upon them."
- Lee Haney

"A person without a sense of humor is like a wagon without springs. It's jolted by every pebble on the road."
- Henry Ward Beecher

"Anyone who stops learning is old, whether at twenty or eighty. Anyone who keeps learning stays young. The greatest thing in life is to keep your mind young."
- Henry Ford

"My formula for living is quite simple. I get up in the morning and I go to bed at night. In between, I occupy myself as best I can."
- Cary Grant

There is always room in your life for thinking bigger, pushing limits and imagining the impossible.
-Tony Robbins

Antar Navigator updated his status: "There is a reality that most are not courageous enough to accept and that is the fact that they were born to be representatives of the Creator. Once that position has been totally accepted and internalized, at that moment the Angels and all of the universal forces accept your command. Many are failures and are living a life of mediocrity and disappointment because they can not conceive of themselves accepting such a high station in life like the one I just described. What I have described is the truth and those who are courageous enough to accept it with courage and the determination to endure, will be victorious beyond the present comprehension of the average and ordinary. The true representatives of the Creator are Above Average and Extra Ordinary, they are indeed the Super Men and the Super Women of our time.".

Antar Navigator updated his status: "Mental and Emotional Highs and lows take place inside of our minds based on how we perceive and react to our inner and outer environment. You have the power to stay on sacred balanced ground mentally and emotionally if you strive hard to learn how to control your mind, your behavior and your reactions to those situations in life that are created by thoughts in and outside of yourself. Once your thoughts are under your control you will find that all of the Chaotic, negative and unproductive thoughts and situations will have their birth in the minds of others. You must discipline your mind to create the mental barrier once and for all that will protect you from the destructive thoughts and ideas of others. Once done you will have Peace, you will have an undisturbed mind with no conflict coming from with in you or from outside of you. This is true freedom (Free-Dome) this is the number one most important goal. This is the true Peace. Peace is first found in the Mind. Stay in the Miracle!".

Antar Navigator updated his status: "Control your thoughts, emotions and behavior. It will be difficult at first but with perfect practice you will become perfect. when you can control your thoughts, your moods and your behavior you have become the Master. Don't live a life where your negative thoughts, emotions and behavior rules you,

Antar Navigator updated his status: "I strive for the ultimate peace, serenity and harmony in my mind. A seed must be planted in fertile soil to achieve proper growth and I require the soil of Peace. Peace is the soil that happiness grows in. No Peace no Happiness. "Stay in the Miracle.""

Courage is never to let your actions be influenced by your fears.
   -Arthur Koestler

Finish each day and be done with it. You have done what you could; some blunders and absurdities have crept in; forget them as soon as you can. Tomorrow is a new day; you shall begin it serenely and with too high a spirit to be encumbered with your old nonsense.
   -Ralph Waldo Emerson

Learn to enjoy every minute of your life. Be happy now. Don't wait for something outside of yourself to make you happy in the future. Think how really precious is the time you have to spend, whether it's at work or with your family. Every minute should be enjoyed and savored.
   -Unknown

"Courage is the most important of all the virtues, because without courage you can't practice any other virtue consistently. You can practice any virtue erratically, but nothing consistently without courage."
   - Maya Angelou

When you give up, when you stop...you're stuck right there. At that point you can only talk about what you used to do...not what you're doing...or what you're planning to do. So stay focused on your goals, PLAN how you're going to reach them, silence and disconnect from the people that make you doubt yourself, keep your eyes open & your mouth shut. Keep it moving so irrelevant people and things can't attach themselves to you. Much love to you and what you strive to do!
Charlene Yedveta Robinson

"He is not wise to me who is wise in words only, but he who is wise in deeds."
   - Saint Gregory

Talent is a gift from God that is within us, do we have to share our talent to the world, or can we keep it for ourselves to share with our loves ones, who decides and gives permission to those who have learn to spread their talent, remember quitters never win and winners never Quit!
   -Al Hajji Robert J. Rowland

If we had a chance to walk outside our body and let your soul wonder, where would you go and who would you see, and how will you pass love on to the Human family!
   - Al Hajji Robert J. Rowland

Why is life so short and the roads we take are very long, what is the reason for life and death, will our souls lay dormant outside this plane on the other side , how many Black on Black crimes will we have before we wake up my people or is it, too late for mankind , will we ever no peace
   -Al Hajji Robert J. Rowland

I been ban from living the American way, just because of my color. Now I denied myself a education, a dream and hope. Where have you been my people, we are in the 21st century. Release the shackles that bound your mind. We are above the despair of the hoods and can achieve anything we put our mind too. Turn the alarm clock on, get up and find away, Al Hajji, May God be with you on your journey

    -Al Hajji Robert J. Rowland

It is 2012,Happy New Year to my children, my friends, my relatives, keep our dreams and aspirations dear to our hearts. Every and anything is possible to achieve no matter what our age. Keep grinding and may God be with us. The spirit of Maat is on our world for 2012 a new beginning for mankind not the ending, all races, religions let us live in peace.

    - Al Hajji Robert J. Rowland

"If a writer knows enough about what he is writing about, he may omit things that he knows. The dignity of movement of an iceberg is due to only one ninth of it being above water."

    - Ernest Hemingway

The way to happiness: Keep your heart free from hate, your mind from worry. Live simply, expect little, give much. Scatter sunshine, forget yourself, and think of others.

    -Norman Vincent Peale

The man who has confidence in himself gains the confidence of others.

    -Hasidic Proverb

I will not die an unlived life. I will not live in fear of falling or catching fire. I choose to inhabit my days, to allow my living to open me, to make me less afraid, more accessible, to loosen my heart until it becomes a wing, a torch, a promise. I choose to risk my ignificance; to live so that which comes to me as seed goes to the next as blossom and that which comes to me as blossom, goes on as fruit.

    -Dawna Markova

The consequences of today are determined by the actions of the past. To change your future, alter your decisions today.
Unknown

"It is not what we get. But who we become, what we contribute... that gives meaning to our lives."
- Tony Robbins

"It takes one person to forgive, it takes two people to be reunited."
- Lewis B. Smedes

Live in the present and make it so beautiful that it will be worth remembering.
-Ida Scott Taylor

To wish you were someone else is to waste the person you are.
-Sven Goran Eriksson

"All our dreams can come true, if we have the courage to pursue them."
- Walt Disney

The optimist sees the rose and not its thorns; the pessimist stares at the thorns, oblivious to the rose.
-Kahlil Gibran

"Even though your kids will consistently do the exact opposite of what you're telling them to do, you have to keep loving them just as much."
- Bill Cosby

"Do not spoil what you have by desiring what you have not; remember that what you now have was once among the things you only hoped for."
- Epicurus

We do not believe in ourselves until someone reveals that deep inside us something is valuable, worth listening to, worthy of our trust, sacred to our touch. Once we believe in ourselves we can risk curiosity, wonder, spontaneous delight or any experience that reveals the human spirit.
  -E.E. Cummings

"Doubt is a pain too lonely to know that faith is his twin brother."
  - Khalil Gibran

"One should not lose one's temper unless one is certain of getting more and more angry to the end."
  - William Butler Yeats

In this life you should read everything you can read. Taste everything you can taste. Meet everyone you can meet. Travel everywhere you can travel. Learn everything you can learn. Experience everything you can experience.
  -Mario Cuomo

"A wise man can learn more from a foolish question than a fool can learn from a wise answer."
  - Bruce Lee

Love and compassion are necessities, not luxuries. Without them humanity cannot survive.
  -Dalai Lama

Have you ever been caught up in the secular world and your spirituality was drain by your ambitions and drive. You look beyond love and the world became your loneliness. While the almighty dollar, became your God.
  -Al Hajji Robert J. Rowland

Remembering you are going to die is the best way I know to avoid the trap of thinking you have something to lose. You are already naked. There is no reason not to follow your heart.
  -Steve Jobs

"The glow of one warm thought is to me worth more than money."
  - Thomas Jefferson

If we can look within and feel the presence of God in our heart.
Then we will be free to create heaven right here at this very moment
in our time on earth.
  -Al Hajji Robert J. Rowland

Remember there are many religions but God called all the prophets
to warn his people, it is time to respect each other's ways.
  -Al Hajji Robert J. Rowland

Champions aren't made in gyms. Champions are made from
something they have deep inside them a desire, a dream, a vision.
They have to have the skill and the will. But the will must be
stronger than the skill.
    -Muhammad Ali

There is no passion to be found playing small, in settling for a life
that is less than the one you are capable of living.
  -Nelson Mandela

Yesterday is history, tomorrow is a mystery. And today? Today is a
gift. That's why we call it the present.
  -B. Olatunji

Antar Navigator updated his status: "We can save our sick world if only we would begin to think properly again. In the medial dorsal nucleus of the thalamus in the brain is where the self is found (1959), attack that region and you destroy the person. No more can we let our children grow up with an inferiority complex. We must at the same time cure those people who possess a superiority complex by alerting them to the fact that it was their past inferiority complex that fueled their present superiority illusion. These mental illnesses are the main problems that are causing the unrest in the world and it can all be traced back to the diabolical manipulation and misuse of the brains of innocent unsuspecting people. So we must save those who reside in a state of inferiority because that mental state is the seed for a future superiority complex that will destroy them completely. Where do we start this process? We start with the removal of all racial images in religion that attempt to portray divinity. Next we censure and control the media images that enter our brain. Last but not least in fact I say it last so it will be first on our minds and that is to remove the conspiracy to reduce the status of women to sex objects who are less than human second class citizens on earth. Once women (the Mothers) are exalted and the mental complexes are removed we will have a state of peace again in our human family."

There is only one word you need to learn and activate to become successful, and that word is 'DO' Every time you are tempted to react in the same old way, ask if you want to be a prisoner of the past or a pioneer of the future.
    -Deepak Chopra

"Be faithful in small things because it is in them that your strength lies."
    -Mother Teresa

Have patience. All things are difficult before they become easy."
    -Saadi

 I find hope in the darkest of days, and focus in the brightest. I do not judge the universe.
- Tenzin Gyatso, the 14th Dalai Lama

Food For Thought

As for those who divide their religion and break up into sects, thou has know part in them in the least. Their affair is with Allah (God). He will in the end, tell them the truth. Surah 6 (chapter 6) Anam, verse 159 The Holy Quran, translator, A Yusuf Ali. In our world today religions are broken down into sects among each major religion. 1. Christianity= Catholics, Baptist, Orthodox Protestant Lutheran, Methodist, Pentecostalism, Mormonism, Jehovah Witness, Presbyterian, Rastafarians, Haitian Vodu, Louisiana Vodoun and Episcopalian and more. 2. Judaism= Ultra-Orthodox/Hassidic, Modern Orthodox Haredi and Chabad. Also Ethnic subdivision Ashkenazic Sefardic Beta Yisrael Mizrahi and Falasha Jews of Ethiopia and more. 3.Islam= Sunni, Sufis, Shia and Ahmaddiya. Also in the middle east the religion of Zoroastrianism. 4.Hindusism= Shaivism, Vaishnavism, Shaktism, Shravtism, and Saurism and more. 5. Buddhism= Theravada, Mahayana, Varayana, and Zen Buddhism 6.Santeria= Tribal Religion of the Yoruba and Bantu people in Southern Nigeria, Cuba, Brazil and other Island still practice the religion. Also, The Ashanti of Central Ghana in Kumasi have a Tribal religion that is a mixture of spiritual and supernatural powers. Human family the last sect or religion I will mention is the worship of Satan 7. Satanism= Laveyan Satanism, Theistic Satanism, Spiritual Satanism, Luciferianism/Gnostic Satanism, and Baphomet Illuminati and more. Satan is the master of confusion and deception. Look at our world, drugs, killings, war, hate. Who is your master and is your sect really involved in the work of Satan? Should we all go back to the pure Hanif doctrine, of Mizraim the first Pharoah (King) of Kemit (Egypt)? He was the second son of Ham. Abraham and Melchizedek, also practiced the Hanif doctrine, to live and die in Faith, in the one true God. In the Hanif doctrine also your spirituality was close to your heart. It became apart of your Ka (in ancient Kemitic/ Egyptian religion, with the ba and the akh, a principal aspect of the soul of a human being or of a god.) Men and Women should never put themselves above another Human Being. We all were equal regardless of race or gender. Let us stop the killing and hating the way others believe in God. In the end as you can see God will judge my friends, our human family. We are one with God and God is in you, if you choose to believe in God and live a good life. The Hanif doctrine or way of life is that simple.

Food For Thought (Cont)

Humans we are made in the image of God and God gave us some of his attributes, to reproduce, think intelligently, control and monitor lower life forms like all the animals on earth. We humans are special on earth and this is our dwelling place. MAAT= Truth, Justice, Peace, Love and Wisdom must return to our planet with the pure true Hanif doctrine. How far must our world go before God restores His order on our and His planet.

Forgive them God for they know not what they do!
Al Hajji Robert J. Rowland.

Un-kept Promises

He said I do for the rest of your life
She said she would be faithful and never sleep with another
Life is full of drama with twist and turns
And in return love has its downfall,
like the waterfalls that run into streams in nature

Un-kept promises
Is there any love left in our world?

He stayed out all night long said he was hanging out with his friends
At the 24 hour night club called Seduction
He should have been at home, because she was entertaining her best male friend. When he got home they were talking on the couch
Looking at each other in their eyes

Un-kept promises
Is there any love left in our world?

Your lady said she would be a character witness for you in your defense. For a trial that was coming up, about you embezzling money from your lady friend. But after further researching on the case, she became the star witness for the prosecution and they found you guilty as charged.

Un-kept promise (Cont)
Un-kept promises
Is there any love left in our world?

He was supposed to meet her for dinner at 6:00pm
But he never showed up. He had a family commitment with his wife
She told him she was trying to get pregnant
In return she was taking her birth control pills everyday
All she wanted was the sex and lust

Un-kept promise
Is there any love left in our world?

Am I Tired

Why can't I get ahead in this game called life?
I move two steps up and the I am four steps back
Trying to move up again, did I release the slaves master shackles
Or am I still bound by the words of my master?
Am I a junkie to my credit card, my alcohol and my pork chops
My white Jesus on the cross, my marijuana, heroin, cocaine
Crack cocaine, my pharmaceutical drugs, and pain medication?
Am I still killing my brothers and sisters because of gang warfare
And he or she wears the wrong color on my turf?
Am I ready to form alliances with African nations
To get back my manhood, my dignity, my right to be a human being?
Am I tired of being misdirected about who I am, and where I come from?
Am I tired of being Racially profiled and mis-treated
Just because of the color of my skin?
Am I tired of praying to a white man on the cross
That they say is Jesus son of God?
Some say God begot none nor was he begotten

AM I Tired (Cont)

Or was Mary really the Theotokos?
No race is superior to another
God should not be made in our images
It creates an inferiority complex on the races or cultures
That are different than the Godly created image.
Am I not in 1825 when slavery was at its peak
Or 1960 when Jim Crow rule the south with separate but equal?
And Black men and women were not considered human beings
It is 2016 and it is time my brothers and sisters, white, yellow
Black or brown. To eradicate all images in the churches depicting
God as being a white man on the cross
If God is omnipotent, omniscient and omnipresent, he is more of a
spirit than flesh
He resides in all creatures, Jinn, Angels and Mankind throughout
our Universe
God is closer to us than our heart beat, God is not about politics and
religionsIn our world today there are different Churches, Mosques,
Temples and Cathedrals
But there is only one God who inspires all religions
Am I the only one who can see?
That it is alright to believe in any religion that fits your need and
soul?
There is only one way and that is to respect our Human Family
To live in peace and harmony
And treat others the way you want to be treated
God is always near, whether we believe or not believe in God

The De – Africanization Of The Ancient Indigenous Kemetic (Egyptian Kushite, Nubian, Kamite) Civilization And People

As The Great Ptahhotep said: If you are an official of high standing, and you are commissioned to satisfy the many, then hold to a straight line. When you speak
Don't lean to one side or to the other. Beware lest someone complain, saying to the judges,
" he has distorted things ", and then your very deeds will turn into a judgment of you.

In the Nile river valley 20,000 years ago? A language in written form came to mankind Mdw Ntr (Mdw Netcher) are the holy writings. They were reveal to the Ancient Kamite
Community. We call these writings Hieroglyphics today, also came the Hieratic – Demotic(Latin) And the Phonetic alphabet today called the Greek alphabet. Black history has been white wash and Arab wash. If you do not know your history, you would believe the Pharaohs of Ancient Kemet were white or Arab. The Ancient Kamite race were black people with knowledge and wisdom, that the world today is still using. The Pharaohs were the guardians of Kemet they were responsible for keeping Maat in Kemet. They were the representative of the God's in Kamite, building temples and communicating with the Gods to keep kemet in order. The Pharaoh was responsible for instructing his people in the reverencing and worship of the gods therefore Maat became a sound foundation for the people. A happy community existed in Kemet, the code of conduct, agriculture and the seven liberal arts were taught to the Kamite people. Grammar, Rhetoric, Logic, Arithmetic
Geometry, Music and Astronomy. The Nile River the longest river in the world 4,145 miles long flowing in Kemet. The pharaoh were responsible for All of Kemet (Africa) and other nations around the world who wanted to follow the Maathain Creed.

The first 20 dynasty of Kemetic Pharaohs were black, and with the invasion of other races and cultural. Miscegenation was in place for the final 15 dynasty of a Pharaohinc democratic Society. Over time Maat dissipated along with the Pharaoh, chaos, greed
New Religions, and new Gods replace a society that man can not pin

point a time of its beginning . Africa since that time has been divided from within and colonialize by European countries. Also remember the Black Egyptian were instrumental in the establishment and writing of the Bible of the New Religion Christianity and Judaism at the Council of Niceae 1 (325 AD), the Council of Constantinople 1 (381 AD), The Council of Ephesus (431 AD), The Council of Chalcedon (451 AD) and the Council of Constantinople 11 (553AD). Also remember that after the Hagia Sophia was completed

(532AD – 537AD). Inside the Hagia Sophia the worlds first academic institution for the Europeans was established. All of the teachers were Black Kemetic (Egyptians) and By the orders of Justinian 1 and his wife Theodora they allowed only young European males to enroll who took the oath of celibacy. The Catholic Christian Church and school was established the young males were instructed in the reverence and worship of God in the new religion and also were taught the seven liberal arts, Grammar, Rhetoric, Logic, Arithmetic, Geometry, Music and Astronomy. They became the Popes, Cardinals and the Priest of the New Churches all over Europe and Modern day Turkey. The Hagia Sophia was the seat of the first Papacy of the Catholic Church.

Between 537AD and 1440 AD, the Anciet Kemet continent became Africa the second

Largest continent with over 11,700,000 square miles. Asia with 17,400,000 square miles

is the largest continent. Africa became divided with over 41 nation states, new religions. As the ARAB SLAVE TRADE.com said : The History of Arab Slavery in Africa 'Alik Shahadah (2002 -2005)

When Islam proliferated in West Africa around the 9th century, one of the first universities was founded by African Muslims. It was called Sankore, Arabs and others came to Sankore which was built in Timbuktu to learn from the African erudites who lectured on Islamic belief, Islamic jurisprudence, astrology, science, and many other subjects. Timbuktu was reputed for African erudition where books and those who traded in books were the wealthiest elites of the merchant society. The bulk of African history after the Ancient Kemetic (Egyptians), Mdw Ntr (Mdw Netcher) , was written in the Arabic language by both Africans and Arabs. The Arabic script also served as an agami to write languages such as Swahili, Wolof and Mande. For thousands of years Arabic served as the international language of trade as English is today. Some of the hidden histories of Africa are locked in as many as 700,000 Arabic manuscripts written by ancient African scholars. One of these the Tariq-ul-Sudan, details the history of Islamic West Africa, but this manuscript remains inaccessible to non-Arabic speakers. A lot Africans became Muslim, because it was close to their indigenous tribal religions. During the 9th century to the 19th century a non chattel slave movement was going on between the Africans and Arab slave traders. Many women stolen from Africa were stolen to serve the infamous Arabian harems; their children were thus born free to Arab fathers and thus would have been heirs to wealth and status, fully and equally assimilated into the population. Their mother's receives the title of "umm walad" (lit. mother of a child), which is an improvement in her status as she can no longer be sold. Among Sunnis, she is automatically freed upon her master's death, however for Shi'a, she is only freed if her child is still alive; her value is then deducted from this child's share of the inheritance.[1] These umm walad, attained "an intermediate position between slave and free" pending their freedom, although they would sometimes be nominally freed as soon as they gave birth. Islam did not outlaw slavery, but Islam did outlaw chattel enslavement. The Koran ask the believers to free their slaves as Atonement for sin. The Koran states " whoever kills his slaves we will kill him". The Koran states " they are your brothers whom Allah placed under your hands. Feed them what you eat, clothe them what you wear and do not impose duties upon them which will over come them. If you so impose duties, then assist them ". Also remember the gold coast of Africa between the 9th century to 1853, Islam was a major religion along with the tribal religions of the region.

From Wikipedia.org The free encyclopedia, Atlantic Slave Trade 1440 – 1853

Spain & Portugal, British, French, and Dutch Traders along with African head of states.

African slaves were destined to Europe, Mexico, Brazil, America and the Caribbean. America had the most cruel form of slavery, chattel enslavement. No human rights, no marriages, babies sold from birth to another slave holder, taken from their mother and father, just another animal on the plantation. As Meltzer stated:

Death in the middle passage of the trans Atlantic trade slave route
was about 2.2 million to 3 million slaves, died
during the voyages between 1440 to 1853. The cramp conditions of
the slave ships and the inhumane treatment of the passenger. They
say over 5 million African slaves died at seasoning camps where
slaves were tortured throughout the Caribbean. Breaking them and
conditioning them to their new lot in life. They say Jamaica held the
most notorious camps and dysentery was the leading cause of death.
Many slaves shipped directly to North
America by passed this process, however most slaves destined for
the Islands or South American plantation, were likely put through
this ordeal. America had its own way to break.

I believe if 7.2 million Africans died the during the crossing and
breaking points and say 15 million were placed into slave labor
throughout the world. A Holocaust took place during this time and
the responsible parties, the European slave traders, plantation
owners and the African head of states for each countries that
provided slave labor. Why want the world leaders or anybody
apologize? Why hasn't any organization or nation step up and
finance a reparation package? Also I believe that the slave trade was
a precursor to colonialism, which was introduced to Africa 30 years
after Brazil outlaw the slave trade in 1853.

In 1883 at the Belgian conference, the interior of Africa was
about to take on a dramatic change. The European leaders had
decided the superior race had to colonialize the heathen Africans.
They realize their natural resources would be a key to the
modernization of the future world. In colonial Africa the history of
the colonist was taught in each country. The Africans were kept in
the dark about their past ancient Kemetic history. To divide and
conquer a people who once rule the world, with their Pharoahinc
Democratic Society. And their religion put mankind on a spiritual
awakening to find solace with God and the mystery of the universe.
The African Continent was transform and to this day the recovery of
the African people is still in jeopardy. The African Continent
remains the only major continent to this day with no national
government set up for the people of the Continent.

The O.A.U. was started after the revolutions in the late 1950's
and early 1960's to free countries from colonial rule. The O.A.U
was the Organization Of African Unity, it was form in 1963 with 33

member African States and by 1973, 8 more independent African States had join. In 2002 the O.A.U. was replaced by the African Union (A.U.) with 53 of the 54 African States as members. The African Union is in the process of trying to unite Africa. But the forces of past economic colonialism, political colonialism, spiritual colonialism, and the lack of education has divided the African people so much. That war, aids, famines and the rape of their natural resources by greedy leaders and their foreign investor from Europe, China, Arabia and America. The manipulate forces which are in place In African Countries (States) , I doubt that I will ever see a United African Continent. But I hope and Pray that with the will of God and our Ancestor, Haile Selassie, Jomo Kenyatta, Kwame Nkrumah, Vizer Ptahhotep, Malcolm X (El - Hajj Malik El - Shabazz), Pharoah Menkauhor, Marcus Garvey, W.E. Dubois, Booker T Washington, Bob Marley, Pharoah Huni, Martin Luther King, Pharoah Seneferu, Elijah Muhammad, Pharoah Khufu, Muammar Al Gaddafi, Stephen Bantu Biko, Patrice Hemery Lumumba   and many others, that our people will wake up from the traps of slavery and colonialism and realize that the unification of Africa will lead to Africa becoming a Super Power.

I hope one day that words can bring peace to a human race that is on the verge of finally figuring out that love is the key to our survival. True history can bring people together to respect each other no matter what their race, religion, skin color or nationality. I have come to the realization that I am a forgiving human being from a loving race of people that have been mis-educated,-misdirected, by controlling industrialist who control the majority of the wealth of our world. Will greed continue to be the criteria of the 5 percent that control 95 percent of the world population. Is it time to pay workers more money, share the wealth my rich brothers. How much profit do you really want to make. Slavery is over humanity is in my brothers, just look within and see, feel and your God will shine the light.

Food For Thought

Universal health care
From Wikipedia, the free encyclopedia

Universal health care – sometimes referred to as universal health coverage, universal coverage, universal care or social health protection - describes health care systems organized around providing a specified package of benefits to all members of a society with the end goal of providing financial risk protection, improved access to health services, and improved health outcomes. Universal health care is not a one-size-fits-all concept; nor does it imply coverage for all people for everything. Universal health care is determined by three critical dimensions: who is covered, what services are covered, and how much of the cost is covered virtually all of Europe has either publicly sponsored and regulated universal health care or publicly provided universal healthcare. The public plans in some countries provide basic or "sick" coverage only; their citizens can purchase supplemental insurance for additional coverage. Countries with universal health care include Austria, Andorra, Belarus, Belgium, Bosnia and Herzegovina, Bulgaria, Croatia, the Czech Republic, Denmark, Estonia, Finland, France, Georgia, Germany, Greece, Hungary, Iceland, Ireland, Italy, Latvia, Liechtenstein, Lithuania, Luxembourg, Malta, Moldova, Monaco, the Netherlands, Norway, Poland, Portugal, Romania, Russia, San Marino, Serbia, Slovakia, Slovenia, Spain, Sweden, Switzerland, Ukraine, and the United Kingdom.

In 1984, the Canada Health Act was passed, which prohibited extra billing by doctors on patients while at the same time billing the public insurance system. In 1999, the prime minister and most premiers reaffirmed in the Social Union Framework Agreement that they are committed to health care that has "comprehensiveness, universality, portability, public administration and accessibility. "The system is for the most part publicly funded, yet most of the services are provided by private enterprises or private corporations, although most hospitals are public. Most doctors do not receive an annual salary, but receive a fee per visit or service. About 29% of Canadians' health care is paid for by the private sector or individuals.] This mostly goes towards services not covered or only partially covered by Medicare such as prescription drugs, dentistry and vision care. Many Canadians have private health insurance, often through their employers, that cover these expenses.

There are more countries around the world with some form of universal health care like Canada, Mexico, Argentina, Chile, Colombia, Peru, Uruguay, Venezuela, Australia, New Zealand, Trinidad, Tobago, Thailand, Republic Of China (Taiwan), Singapore, People's Republic Of China, Macau, Israel, India, Hong Kong, Algeria, Egypt, Ghana, Libya, South Africa, and Morocco. Our country America has no Universals Health Care Plan. The United States does not have a universal health care system, however the Patient Protection and Affordable Care Act (PPACA) as amended by the Health Care and Education Reconciliation Act of 2010, seeks to have expanded insurance coverage to legal residents by 2014. It provides for federally mandated health insurance to be implemented in the United States during the 2010–2019 decade with the Federal government subsidizing legal resident households with income up to 400% of the Federal poverty level.

But as I am writing this Friday June 29th the Supreme Court will decide the faith of the PPACA. I was just thinking All of our elected officials in Washington, Senators and House of Representatives enjoy great health care benefits. And the thing about it is that taxpayer dollars are paying for the majority of their benefits. But somehow another these same elected officials want to call President Obama, Patient Protection and Affordable Care Act (PPACA), Obama Care.

But over half of the world has some form of Universal Health Care. Congress has their own Pharmacy right in the capitol, Doctors, Nurses or on call seconds away, X ray machines, Electrocardiogram and technicians are available right there in the capitol. I know pharmaceutical companies, health care providers, and insurance companies are major lobbyist in Washington D.C. They are putting 100 Millions of dollars and more in elected officials campaign funds. Do you know that in 2004 the Medicare Reform Act, Medicare is prohibited from negotiating with pharmaceuticals companies for lower prices. This act was passed by a Republican President and a Bipartisan congress. Why has congress not passed laws to help the poor get insurance in our country. They would rather spend the taxpayer money on weapons and bailing out Wall Street and Banks. Our insurance rates keep going up our citizen are receiving piss poor health care. A lot of our bankruptcy, are medical related with astronomical medical bills. I wonder sometimes or our doctors for greed or is it still a healing profession to heal the sick and wounded, physically and mentally. And our congress is way out of touch of the people needs. I think America really does need a Universal Health Care Plan, wake up America the dream is over, let us face reality.

Food For Thought

African American consumer spent $ 1.04 trillion dollars in 2011. The Gross Domestic Product (GDP) at Purchasing Power Parity (PPP) according to the International Monetary Fund, figures are given in 2010 International dollars. The number 1 African rank country and 25th world rank country South Africa DDP (PPP) was $523.954 Billion dollars and the 2nd rank country and 26th world rank country Egypt GDP (PPP) was $497.781 Billion dollars. The United States economy is the world's largest National economy, with an estimated 2011 GDP (PPP) of $15.1 trillion dollars. The African American GDP (PPP) in 2011 spending $1.04 trillion dollars, would have rank us 16th in the world behind South Korea, 15th rank in the world With a GDP (PPP) at 1.116.247 trillion dollars.

African Americans if you realize it or not you are being marketed, by car companies, insurance companies, food & drink companies and more. Check out Black Consumers.com it is full of data and strategies to help brands reach black consumers. It is time for us to spend and support our owned Black business. Set up business relationship in African countries to distribute finish goods for import and export. Also we need to support the existing black owned banks and established more black banks.

We need to set up more mentoring programs and Tutorial programs in the African American Communities our drop out rate in the public high schools are still to high nationally. We need to established Pen Pals, E-mail Pals to African countries and start pushing for the unification of the African Continent. A united Africa would strengthing the Global Economy and bring the world closer to a peaceful co-existence. One currency for 61 African states (countries) 1 President, 61 Governors, 122 senators, 360 or more house of representatives a Democratic peaceful African Union. African Americans, we also need to help in eradicating illiteracy and poverty in Africa. Almost 60per cent of the African people are illiterate and 45percent of the African people live in poverty. It is our time to reach out to Africa. If Africa is not united then African Americans will never be united.

"Throughout history, it has been the inaction of those who could have acted, the indifference of those who should have known better, the silence of the voice of justice when it mattered most, that has made it possible for evil to triumph".
 - Haile Selassie

Famous Quotes

You've been given the innate power to shape your life...but you cannot just speak change, you have to LIVE change. Intent paired with action builds the bridge to success. You can't just want it; you have to do it, live it...BE it! Success isn't something you have, it's something you DO!
   -STEVE MARABOLI

"The ultimate measure of a man is not where he stands in moments of comfort and convenience, but where he stands at times of challenge and controversy."
   -Martin Luther King, Jr.

We make such messes in this life, both accidently and on purpose. But wiping the surface clean doesn't really make anything any neater. It just masks what is below. It's only when you really dig down deep, go underground, that you can see who you really are.
   -Sarah Dessen

When I understand myself, I understand you, and out of that understanding comes love. Love is the missing factor; there is a lack of affection, of warmth in relationship; and because we lack that love, that tenderness, that generosity, that mercy in relationship, we escape into mass action which produces further confusion, further misery. We fill our hearts with blueprints for world reform and do not look to that one resolving factor which is love.
   -Jiddu Krishnamurti

"Death is no more than passing from one room into another. But there's a difference for me, you know. Because in that other room I shall be able to see."
   -Helen Keller

Your work is going to fill a large part of your life, and the only way to be truly satisfied is to do what you believe is great work. And the only way to do great work is to love what you do.If you haven't found it yet, keep looking. Don't settle.
-Steve Jobs

Count your blessings. Once you realize how valuable you are and how much you have going for you, the smiles will return, the sun will break out, the music will play, and you will finally be able to move forward the life that God intended for you with grace, strength, courage, and confidence.
-Og Mandino

"We must use time wisely and forever realize that the time is always ripe to do right."
- Nelson Mandela

If you were all alone in the universe with no one to talk to, no one with which to share the beauty of the stars, to laugh with, to touch, what would be your purpose in life? It is other life; it is love, which gives your life meaning. This is harmony. We must discover the joy of each other, the joy of challenge, the joy of growth.
-Mitsugi Saotome

A man is like a novel: until the very last page you don't know how it will end. Otherwise it wouldn't be worth reading.
-Yevgeny Zamyatin

We cannot have the oppressors telling the oppressed how to rid themselves of the oppressor
— Kwame Ture

We never know when our last day on earth will be. So, love with full sincerity, believe with true faith, and hope with all of your might. Better to have lived in truth and discovered life, than to have lived half heartedly, and died long before you ever ceased breathing.
-Cristina Marrero

The ability to discipline yourself to delay gratification in the short term in order to enjoy greater rewards in the long term, is the indispensable prerequisite for success.
-Brian Tracy

Never stop just because you feel defeated. The journey to the other side is attainable only after great suffering
-Santosh Kalwar

When you arise in the morning, think of what a precious privilege it is to be alive - to breathe, to think, to enjoy, to love - then make that day count!
-Steve Maraboli

Give yourself entirely to those around you. Be generous with your blessings. A kind gesture can reach a wound that only compassion can heal.
-Steve Maraboli

Forget yesterday - it has already forgotten you. Don't sweat tomorrow - you haven't even met. Instead, open your eyes and your heart to a truly precious gift - today.
--Steve Maraboli

Even though you may want to move forward in your life, you may have one foot on the brakes. In order to be free, we must learn how to let go. Release the hurt. Release the fear. Refuse to entertain your old pain. The energy it takes to hang onto the past is holding you back from a new life. What is it you would let go of today?
-Mary Manin Morrissey

No longer must the African genius be trapped between bureaucracy and mismanagement
– Alik Shahadah

Injustice anywhere is a threat to justice everywhere.
– Martin L. King, Jr

If we stand tall it is because we stand on the shoulders of many ancestors.
— African Proverb

Trust...
"Trust is the glue of life. It's the most essential ingredient in effective communication. It's the foundational principle that holds all relationships."
- Stephen R. Covey

Dreams..."Every great dream begins with a dreamer. Always remember, you have within you the strength, the patience, and the passion to reach for the stars to change the world."
- Harriet Tubman

Carry out a random act of kindness, with no expectation of reward, safe in the knowledge that one day someone might do the same for you.
- Diana Spencer

Secret Societies Around Our World

Mankind has been engaged in studying mysteries of life since the beginning of time. Praying to a God the Creator and getting in tune with our spirit, Ka, soul, to make us better human beings, on our time in this earthly plane. The Creator through His cosmic forces has sent many prophets, messiah, wise men and women to help develop each and every one of us individually. It is not a coincidence that each person that is a life force on this planet, comes through the woman's vagina and a man's sperm planted the seed inside to create this life. So what do secret societies conceal? Are they protecting the lies of the religions on our planet? Are they protecting a plot for a New World Order? Are they evil and Satan is their Master Mind? Are they helping to uplift the Human race?

There are many Secret Societies and some have overlapped with each other. Some are lost never to be found again. Some are right in front of us every day working to conceal and hide information. To keep the common people squabbling over their religions about who is right and what is wrong. I will list some of the Secret Societies I have run across in my research. It is up to you to read about them. One more question for you! Are the modern day religious organizations Catholicism, Judaism, Islamism, Buddhism, Hinduism, Zoroastrianism, Christianism, Protestantism, are they secret Societies? Here are a list of Secret Societies I have found.

SCAN – Secret Coalition for American Nationalism

Skull and Bones – Yale University Fraternal Club

The Vatican – The Catholic Church

The Free Masons

The Illuminati

The Rosicrucian Order

The Knights Templar

The Bilderberg Group

Opus Dei

The Knights Of Malta

The Priory Of Sion

CFR – The Council On Foreign Relations

C.I.A. – Central Intelligent Agency

F.B.I. – Federal Bureau Of Investigation

T.C. – Trilateral Commission

Gnostics

Cathars

Bohemian Grove

New World Order

Secret Service

President – Commander and Chief of the United States

Grand Lodge Of Luxor – Ancient Lower and Upper Egypt - subordinate lodges around the world

Shriners – Ancient Arabic Order Of The Nobles Of The Mystic Shrine

Luciferism

Black Boule'

Knights Of St. Peter Claver

Plum Island

Area 51

Majestic 12

What Human kind has in common is that God is within us and not our Religion. The only right order is God's Light. Let us live in peace not war. May God be with each and every one of us regardless of race, religion and country of origin.

One Love, Al Hajji Robert J. Rowland,
Peace my people!

" Two Steps Up "

Me and my lady, we like to go out and dance
It is a way that we can romance each other
Our dancing is simple like her smile
And the lines in her dimples, yeah

Chorus
Two steps up, Two steps back
Bring her close and turn her around
We gonna two step

When we get home, we like to burn some candles
She allows me to handle the moment
I put on some Isley brothers slow jams
We cuddle up to each other like some college lovers

Chorus
Two steps up, Two steps back
Bring her close and turn her around
We gonna two step

We are so close and in our beds tonight
I will love her right, cause I know what she likes
The baby making music is in the air
As I run my fingers over her thighs to her hair

Chorus
Two steps up, Two steps back
Bring her close and turn her around
We gonna two step

" *The Other Side Of Life*"

I was on the other side of life
And my world is upside down
I got to go to work and do my job
No more road trips and hanging out back stage
While the show was going on
I was on the other side of life
And now I watch my young son grow
Spending time with him, when his momma said so
Hoping we can bond in our short time we spend together
I was on the other side of life
And now freedom is within my sight
People we are not the judge or the jury
We hold the keys to our destiny
With preparation and a lot of hard work
I was on the other side of life
I remember working for free, no pay, no rights, I was just here
I learned to read and write and I fought for my dreams
How I ended up smoking and not giving a damn
I don't remember, I thought I could see what was ahead of me
I was on the other side of life

Bear My Arms

Gun shots ring in the air

A misogynist on the loose

He is in an elementary school

Shooting kids with a AR 15 assault weapon

26 die including him at that spot

His mother shot at home and she was left to die

A mixed up human being has misinformed his friends

An irreversible action took place in time

Where violence seems to ring supreme

Should I postpone my gun purchase?

I do not have one yet

I think I need to exercise my second amendment rights

I have the right to bear my arms

Change My Ways

My bed was empty I was all alone tonight
I took a one on one of some cocaine up my nose
From the mirror sitting on the bed stand
had a glass of Cognac in one hand ready to take a sip.
Would I be able to change my ways?
Would I be able to rearrange my life?
Would I be able to walk a straight line?
Would I be able to live up to my part?
Should I call up a party woman friend of mine
She was two doors down from me in apartment number 69
My main woman left yesterday she packed up her things
Said she needed a husband not a hustler and a want to be
Player.
Would I be able to change my ways?
Would I be able to rearrange my life?
Would I be able to walk a straight line?
Would I be able to live up to my part?
I wanted to get on my knees and beg her please don't leave
I had a few words for God please watch over me
She was such a lady with so much class and grace
I thought for a moment she deserved better than me
Would I be able to change my ways?
Would I be able to rearrange my life?
Would I be able to walk a straight line?
Would I be able to live up to my part?
I decided to call my woman and ask her
When she was coming home. I told her I needed her
Tonight and the rest of my life, please come home
I know we can work it out. There was a knock at the door
And my woman was standing there.
Would I be able to change my ways?
Would I be able to rearrange my life?
Would I be able to walk a straight line?
Would I be able to live up to my part?

Un Safe Gold Mine

Poverty sometimes make you do things to survive!

Like working as an artisanal gold miner not authorized or supervised

I think I am a entrepreneur using my own tools of my trade

But the soil I work in is tainted with lead, killing me, my fathers, my

mothers and my children

Children are blind, paralyzed, and have serious nerve damage

In Bagega, Nigeria, 1,010 children will have treatment to hopefully

dissolve the lead. When will greed not be the criteria of mankind's

heart? And when will we learn to share and dare to be right?

Oh God forgive us and keep us on a straight path in this life.

  Dedicated to the children of Bagega, Nigeria God have mercy

"Waiting For You"

You and I have crossed many paths

We have searched for God in all His houses

To find his original plan for mankind.

Crossing ocean on ships and then by air.

Oh yeah, we met before talked and laughed

And we held mother Kemit (Africa) dear to our souls.

We departed friends with like minds.

You went on your journey and I went on mine.

Now we cross path again talking, laughing and texting.

My lady friend God is guiding us to love.

Can we open our hearts up to love again?

Hearing your voice makes me happy my friend!

Especially on days when I seem I am all alone.

This is God talking to me through my third eye.

It is our journey just wait and see woman.

Just look down the road and you will.

See me standing there waiting for you.

Food for thought

May the light of God Shine on our souls
And may the mercy of God envelop Mankind
And Heal us of our past transgression

Al Hajji Robert J Rowland

Neo-Liberalism

Control by corporate financial elite (lobbyist)
It has disable and renew economic equality for the masses
Created a new form of racism with government intervention
Retrench Voting Rights and Affirmative Action
Racial Disparity 28% African American, live below the poverty line
Economic inequality, Racial inequality, Racial profiling ,
Mass incarceration of African American
Segregated schools in the inner cities
Distrust in Government Homicide increases
Homicide rates between 1971-2013 have peak for African American
African American on African American Homicide has increase

America has the most church going people and believers of God.
It also has the most homicide in the world today.
Are our religions man made or God made.
Where is the love of mankind in our churches

Neter (The one supreme power God Of Ancient Kemit (Africa)

Not known are the things which will do God
Thou shall not cause terror in men and women
The eating of bread is according to the plan of God
If thou are a farmer and labor in the field which God has given thee
If thou wouldst be like a wise man make thou son to be pleasing
unto God

Satisfy those who depend on thee
So far as it may be done by thee
It should be done by those favored of God
Who have become the guardian of the provisions of God

What is loved of God is obedience, disobedience hated God
The house of God what it hates is to much speaking a loose tongue
Pray thou with a loving heart the petitions of which all are in secret
He will do thy business, He will hear that which thou sayest.
And will accept thine offerings giveth thy God existence
Thy God will judge the right in offerings to thy God
Guard thou against the things which he abominated/

Satisfy those who depend on thee
So far as it may be done by thee
It should be done by those favored of God
Who have become the guardian of the provisions of God

O behold with thine eyes his plans devote thy self to adore his name
Neter
It is he who giveth souls to millions of forms and he magnifieth who
so ever magnifieth him
Now the God of this earth is Neter, who is the ruler of the horizon
If she thy mother raiseth her hands to God he will hear her prayer
and rebuke thee Satan
Give thyself to God, keep thyself daily for God and let tomorrow be
as today

Neter (Cont)

Satisfy those who depend on thee
So far as it may be done by thee
It should be done by those favored of God
Who have become the guardian of the provisions of God

From Papyrus of Ani (aka "The Egyptian Book Of The Dead")

Famous Quotes

The finish line is just the beginning of a whole new race.
— Unknown

Strength does not come from physical capacity. It comes from an indomitable will.
— Mahatma Gandhi

Ability is what you're capable of doing. Motivation determines what you do. Attitude determines how well you do it.
— Lou Holtz

"If instead of a gem, or even a flower, we should cast the gift of a loving thought into the heart of a friend, that would be giving as the angels give."
— George MacDonald

An idea that is developed and put into action is more important than an idea that exists only as an idea.
— Buddha

A good friend is a connection to life, a tie to the past, a road to the future, the key to sanity in a totally insane world.
— Lois Wyse

Our soul desires to be understanding, our ego is only concerned with being understood. When you are being understanding you are connected to your soul.
— Michaiel Bovenes

Nature, by example, shows us anything worthwhile comes over time. Anything worthwhile grows methodically, building on a strong foundation. Develop a willingness to carry on despite roadblocks.
— Jaren L. Davis

"The fish trap exists because of the fish. Once you've gotten the fish you can forget the trap. The rabbit snare exists because of the rabbit. Once you've gotten the rabbit, you can forget the snare. Words exist because of meaning. Once you've gotten the meaning, you can forget the words. Where can I find a man who has forgotten words so I can talk with him?"
— Chuang Tzu

Do the one thing you think you cannot do. Fail at it. Try again. Do better the second time. The only people who never tumble are those who never mount the high wire. This is your moment. Own it.
— Oprah Winfrey

More Famous Quotes
"People will forget what you said. But people will never forget how you made them feel."
  - Maya Angelou

"If you find someone who makes you smile, who checks up on you often to see if you're okay, who watches out for you and wants the very best for you, don't let them go. Keep them close and don't take them for granted. People like that are hard to find."
— Unknown

Humankind has not woven the web of life. We are but one thread within it. Whatever we do to the web, we do to ourselves. All things are bound together. All things connect.
— Chief Seattle

The vision that you glorify in your mind, the ideal that you enthrone in your heart - this you will build your life by, and this you will become.
— James Allen

To be capable of steady friendship or lasting love, are the two greatest proofs, not only of goodness of heart, but of strength of mind.
— Paul Aubuchon

Greatness...

"The greatness of a man is not in how much wealth he acquires, but in his integrity and his ability to affect those around him positively."
— Bob Marley

Responsibility...
"You must take personal responsibility. You cannot change the circumstances, the seasons, or the wind, but you can change yourself. That is something you have charge of."
— Jim Rohn

Embrace the faith that every challenge surmounted by your energy; every problem solved by your wisdom; every soul stirred by your passion; and every barrier to justice brought down by your determination will ennoble your own life, inspire others, serve your country, and explode outward the boundaries of what is achievable on this earth.
— Madeleine Albright

Food For Thought

In My book " From The Hood To The Holy Land And Back Plus More" chapter 14, "Do We Know What We Eat?" I talk about Genetically modified food, Genetically engineered foods. The use of steroid hormones for growth promotion in food producing animals and our diet leading us to medical issue. Did you know that Soy bean is a biotech food crop that has been Genetically modified. Jo Miles of Food & Water watch sent me this E-Mail about the Farm Bill that is in Congress this is a tidbit of the E-mail. "I know that you care about the food your family eats, and where it comes from. You can be sure that corporations like Monsanto are pressuring Congress to pass a Farm Bill that's friendlier to them, and extremists are fighting to get rid of food stamps. That's why your voice is so important. Let your Members of Congress know that you want a Farm Bill that protects ordinary Americans, not big corporations.

Join me in calling for a better Farm Bill:
https://secure3.convio.net/fww/site/Advocacy?pagename=homepage&page=UserAction&id=973

" Food For Thought "

If you have not heard there will be a permanent memorial at the United Nations remembering the Trans-Atlantic Slave Trade and its African victims. A unveiling ceremony of the model and the designer Haitian American Rodney Leon, took place on Sept 23 at UN headquarters in New York. UN Secretary-General Ban Ki-Moon, said the memorial "will serve as a reminder of the bravery of those slaves, abolitionists and unsung heroes who managed to rise up against an oppressive system, fight for their freedom and end the practice." Mr. Leon, a Manhattan based architect known for his design of the African Burial Ground Memorial in lower Manhattan. He said "The Ark of Return" is a educational tool, not just a memorial. "I designed the Ark of Return as a sacred space to psychologically and spiritually transport visitors to the United Nations to a place where acknowledgement, education, reflection and healing can take place. Our design will allow people to learn of the tragedy of the Trans -Atlantic Slave Trade and its Global scale. I want the memorial to be something that invokes memory, almost a ritualistic experience, the image needs to be very powerful so I developed the triangular concept of the ship from the historic triangle created by the middle passage, the human sized figure of a body laying horizontally as almost suspended in air to communicate the horror endured by the millions of African people during the Middle Passage. And the reflecting pool known as ' Lest We Forget' with a three dimensional map with Africa at its center, allows for our spirits to enter the traditional African rituals of prayer and Libation". The progress of construction on the Memorial, expected to be completed in the autumn of 2014, can be followed via @RememberSlavery on Twitter and facebook.com/rememberslavery. Updates will also be posted from the Permanent Memorial Committee via their Facebook page.

Remember Slavery

Famous Quotes

A lie can travel half way around the world while the truth is putting on its shoes."
— Charles Spurgeon

Food For Thought

Secession took place during the civil war, when southern states withdrew from the federal union. Why are these same states still producing prejudice and close minded individuals? As Warren Buffet put it, "Inequality in the economic distribution of wealth in America is our last hurdle as a true democracy. Government will have to intercede in this process with entitlement payments until the gap is closed". Welfare, Social Security, Medicaid, Medicare, and T.A.R.P, Payments (Troubled Asset Relief Program) TARP allowed the United States Department of the Treasury to purchase or insure up to $700 billion of "troubled assets," defined as "(A) residential or commercial mortgages and any securities, obligations, or other instruments that are based on or related to such mortgages, that in each case was originated or issued on or before March 14, 2008, the purchase of which the Secretary determines promotes financial market stability; and (B) any other financial instrument that the Secretary, after consultation with the Chairman of the Board of Governors of the Federal Reserve System, determines the purchase of which is necessary to promote financial market stability, but only upon transmittal of such determination, in writing, to the appropriate committees of Congress."[4]
In short, this allows the Treasury to purchase illiquid, difficult-to-value assets from banks and other financial institutions. The targeted assets can be collateralized debt obligations, which were sold in a booming market until 2007, when they were hit by widespread foreclosures on the underlying loans. TARP is intended to improve the liquidity of these assets by purchasing them using secondary market mechanisms, thus allowing participating institutions to stabilize their balance sheets and avoid further losses.
TARP does not allow banks to recoup losses already incurred on troubled assets, but officials expect that once trading of these assets

resumes, their prices will stabilize and ultimately increase in value, resulting in gains to both participating banks and the Treasury itself. The concept of future gains from troubled assets comes from the hypothesis in the financial industry that these assets are oversold, as only a small percentage of all mortgages are in default, while the relative fall in prices represents losses from a much higher default rate. Tarp also allowed the bail out of Wall Street and the American Car industry. Right now the Federal Government, is in another crisis and a majority group in congress wants to pass short term funding and continued a sequestration policy that is very irresponsible. One thing Warren Buffet overlooked is that just because your eyes are open it does not make you see what your fellow man and woman sees. We are all molded by our environments and our household philosophies. Let there be peace on our planet, diplomacy not war.

God be with us Al Hajji Robert J. Rowland

Food For Thought

Oct 1st, the implementation of the Affordable Care Act or the Right Wing terminology Obama Care, is supposed to take effect in all 50 states and territory of the USA. Obstructionist in some states are trying to repeal this Federal Law. We my people are in the 21st century not the 20th century. It is time for America to be a true Democracy and Include 85 % of the people in the distribution of wealth. With New Wages, New Educational Systems, New Health Care Reform and etc. Greed is a disease not a medicine to heal our country. The Right Wing and their lobbyist are trying to stick America up and cause the break up of one of the greatest countries this planet has been blessed with. Wake up people, this is not about the color of your skin. This is about control of the poor and middle class people to be their pawns and continue for us to work for meager wages and tax us to finance and purchase the goods and services of the elite few. Also my fellow Americans the funding of our Federal Government is in the hands of these Right Wing Republicans in the House Of Representative who want to cut spending and repeal Welfare, Social Security, Environmental

Protection Agency, The Regulation Of Wall Street and Oil Companies. If The Federal Government does not have a budget, how many bills can we pay? None I assume. The Right Wing has become the Wrong Wing in America. Can they not see it is time to do the Right things?

Peace, God have mercy on my country, Al Hajji Robert J. Rowland

Food For Thought

To all human kind. Pig (Swine) meat is causing a epidemic bringing havoc on the masses of people. High blood pressure, obesity, cancer, diabetes, lymphoma and etc. The dietary laws of the Prophets and Messiah God sent to all religions, pork was excluded from the menu. Adam, Noah, Enoch, Abraham, Isaac, Shuaib, Jacob(Israel) Akhenaten, Moses, Salih, David, Solomon, Ptah Hotep, Jesus, Buddah, Vishnu and Mohammed never ate pork. In Ancient kemit (Egypt Africa) and Biblical Jerusalem, pigs were put in garbage pits to eat the garbage. When the pigs stop eating the garbage after becoming excessively fat, the pits and pigs were set on fire and new pigs entered. There were no diseases in Ancient Kemit (Egypt Africa) and Biblical Jerusalem that were food related. In the Holy Bible in St Matthew chapter 8, 28-32 pigs were used to capture demonic (devilish) spirits. Remember because something that taste good might not be good for you.

Al Hajji Robert J. Rowland, One God love

Famous Quotes

When we feel love and kindness toward others, it not only makes others feel loved and cared for, but it helps us also to develop inner happiness and peace.
— The 14th Dalai Lama

At the end of your life, you will never regret not having passed one more test, not winning one more verdict, or not closing one more deal. You will regret time not spent with a husband, a friend, a child, or a parent.
— Barbara Bush

"No one saves us but ourselves. No one can and no one may. We ourselves must walk the path."
— Buddha

I like your Christ, I do not like your Christians. Your Christians are so unlike your Christ.
-Mahatma Gandhi

I believe in human beings, and that all human beings should be respected as such, regardless of their color
-El-Hajj Malik- El Shabazz (Malcolm X)

"Darkness cannot drive out darkness: only light can do that. Hate cannot drive out hate: only love can do that."
— Martin Luther King, Jr.

Will our people ever wake up to see who we really are a proud people a loving people, a caring people, a God fearing people, a just people in tune to the cosmic forces of the universe. Human family there is too much violence on our planet, too much hate on our planet, to many racist on our planet, not enough love on our planet, let us look within our hearts and let it weigh our decision.
-Al Hajji Robert J. Rowland

If God is watching over us right now, in your place, your body, your mind, is not your religion a way of life.
-Al Hajji Robert J. Rowland

Be Yourself...
 "Be who you are and say what you feel, because those who mind don't matter and those who matter don't mind."
— Dr. Seuss

Food For Thought

To the Jihadist or to Jihad, remember Jihad is an Arabic word meaning to struggle, to defend your character, to defend your religion. The highest form of Jihad is to fight in battle if your enemy attacks you with the intent of taking your life and trying to destroy your nation, community of brothers, sisters and family of Islam, Judaism, Christianity and whatever your religion might be. The main purpose of Jihad was the everyday struggle of life, to make my prayers to God, to refrain from lust, adultery, fornication, drinking alcohol, gambling, lying, stealing, using and selling drugs. As you can see we all will fall short of the true Jihad no one is perfect and God has given us the choice to choose any of his major books and Prophets. They all ask us to treat someone the way you wanted be treated. I am not the judge of no man and his action but remember there is an enemy lurking where ever there is good and Satan is in his spirit.

Al Hajji Robert J. Rowland

Food For Thought

Human family let us not forget about Trayvon Martin. Let us not see color. Let every child grow to become a man or a woman. Stop hate subconsciously, Logically, and illogically. Let us take a stand on understanding our human family, peace, love and hand in your guns. It is time to start having some fun. If you need a gun, a friend of mine Bobby Carswell suggested we have a national rent your Gun stores. Keep them a week to hunt if you are in the rural areas in America or target and skeet shooting in the cities. Turn your gun in and go back and rent again when needed. The right to bare arms came with the 2nd amendment in 1791 with single shot muskets we have automatic guns that can fire 200 rounds in a minute and weapons of mass destruction that can leave buildings standing but decimate humans by the millions. If you are caught with a gun 10 years in prison. NRA get out of Washington DC. you have bought enough politicians to keep violence on the streets. Spend some money on the abolishment of the second amendment. We are in the year 2013. Are you not tired of supporting barbaric attitudes? I have an 16 year old son, a 17 year old nephew and a 15 year old grandson. They all could have been Trayvon. Let us stand our ground and turn in some guns.
AL Hajji Robert J. Rowland Peace and God Love

Food For Thought

On July 12, 1887, the city of Mound Bayou, Mississippi was founded by Isaiah T. Montgomery and his cousin, Benjamin T. Green, former slaves of Joseph Emory Davis. Mound Bayou is situated halfway between Vicksburg, Mississippi and Memphis, Tennessee off of Highway 61. These slaves however, were born into a family that ran the business sector of one of the largest and enterprising plantation in that area of the country. Montgomery's father, Benjamin Montgomery was the contributing factor behind the successful mastermind of the Davis' notable enterprise. Mound Bayou remains the oldest bastion of Black municipal government in the South. Isaiah T. Montgomery and Benjamin T. Green had as their dream since before the Civil War to found the largest U.S.

Negro Town. Montgomery and Green founded, Mound Bayou to serve as a sanctuary for African-American families and culture. Throughout the years, Mound Bayou has continued its long tradition of community self-empowerment that has produced numerous African American leaders, innovators, and proud family lineages. Mound Bayou has always been a model city for the capabilities of African-Americans to rise above inequality in the South. The town has never practiced or experienced segregation within its borders. Mound Bayou is a town without second class citizen. In 1890 did the Mississippi constitutional convention lead to Jim Crow in The south? Here is an account of the convention which led to the death of a white representative Marsh Cook.

During the 1890 Constitutional Convention in Jackson, Mississippi, two men, at least, seemed to be on the wrong sides of the color line; Marsh Cook, a white Republican from Jasper County, and Isaiah T. Montgomery, eventually the only black representative at the convention, stood up for things taboo to many in their respective communities. The results of each man's stand not only affected them personally, but also shaped the future of Mississippi for many years to come. Cook and Montgomery looked back at the years after the Civil War and preceding the 1890 convention and saw the same thing. In 1875, after ten years of Republicans in Mississippi joining forces with blacks, scalawags, and carpetbaggers, resulting in what many white Mississippians referred to as negro rule, it was apparently decided, according to Dunbar Rowland, that the negro has proven himself unworthy of suffrage, and it should be taken from him. Following an apparently very bloody revolution in which whites took back control (in theory), 15 years of intimidation passed, during which according to James George as printed in the Jackson Clarion Ledger, the method of preserving white supremacy was never entirely satisfactory. Isaiah Montgomery, in his speech during the 1890 convention, described these years in terms of every form of [political] demoralization [for blacks]-bloodshed, bribery, [and] ballot stuffing. Although the convention took place under the pretext of, according to Rowland, eliminating ignorance at the ballot box, it was in fact a move to lawfully disenfranchise a majority of black voters by using a poll tax and a literary test in order to establish franchise qualification. According to estimates by Montgomery, the new State Constitution would disenfranchise 11,889 whites and 123,334 blacks in Mississippi. The Cleveland Gazette hoped the unconstitutional and un-American action would be prevented or at least delayed a few years, but it was not to be. For his part, and against what would perhaps be expected of a white Mississippian, Marsh Cook, according to an online PBS history of Jim Crow, took a stand against the principles of the gathering delegation and courageously challenged the Democrats for a seat to the Constitutional Convention in spite of death threats. Isaiah Montgomery did the opposite. As the only black representative to the convention, he took the opportunity to appeal to the good natures of the white representatives and their belief in a Supreme Arbiter, which supposedly would help the two races march together towards new and greater triumphs of progressive civilization. Montgomery apparently recognized the legitimacy of the white demand to rule for their [the whites] own protection, and he foolishly [in retrospect] hoped, by his support of the new constitution and its subsequent passing, that he and other black Mississippians would gain favor in white sight, thus bridging a chasm that has been widening and deepening for a generation He hoped his appeals would lead to the death of the constitutional movement or perhaps, if it passed, an immediate reversal of the new constitution. Both men failed. Marsh Cook was ambushed and murdered, according to PBS, on a lonely road. The Cleveland Gazette hoped that his murder, being that of a respectable white gentleman, would cause the federal government to take the necessary steps to protect the American citizen at home, be his color what it may. It did not. Montgomery's hopes of racial cooperation also did not materialize. He was lambasted by the Cleveland Gazette, which called his defense of the monstrous franchise provision...a disgrace to the race and to our civilization, and wished he had never been born. For all of their objections, however, Mississippi, and the rest of the South, as many other states followed suit, plunged itself headfirst into a half-century of legal disenfranchisement and discrimination.

Per Wikipedia

Food For Thought

Deneen Borelli a black female, author of " Blacklash" considers the book as a call to action to empower Americans to help stop the cycle of government dependency, which deprives citizens of their rights to freedom and prosperity. She said, one thing I realized, especially within the black community, is that there is a monopoly on the message. The monopoly is generally from the black establishment—I'm talking about Jesse Jackson, Al Sharpton, different black publications. They're all saying pretty much the same thing, and it's not really a message of liberty, it's not really a message of personal responsibility. Sadly, we have this message of victimization, and times that blacks need special treatment when, in fact, that's all a lie. That is why I can speak from experience, to say that it's a lie. So I implore anyone—but especially our young black youth, and anyone in the black community—to, please, do your research. Don't just follow the crowd! Learn on your own, and then make an informed decision. That is really how I got to the point where I am today Fixation On Victimization. My question to Deneen, Are we African American acting like victims? Are we the victims of race haters who have no clue of how to include all of humanity in the American dream. Deneen believes if African American become more responsible in the class room while attending class. They will be better off educating themselves in High School and the university systems attaining a trade or a degree. She believes African American are not victims of society. She also believes that there should be no affirmative action or quoted system. She believes 400 years of slavery and Jim Crow between 1890 and 1968 in the southern states should be no excuse for playing the race card. Deneen ask what are some solutions to eradicate teen pregnancy, high school drop outs, illegal drug pushing in the hoods, single parent households, S.T.D. and gangs in our hoods. She also believes that African Americans rely on entitlement programs like welfare and disability which has risen over the last 10 years.

Sometime I wonder 300 to 400 years of servitude in the longest lasting industry in America, slavery and free labor. Deneen the effect of slavery are all around us in our hoods, Gangs, drugs, killings, poverty, mental health and the highest incarceration rate of any ethnic group in America. Deneen do we lived in hoods? Yes Deneen Are we victims of our hoods? Yes

Food For Thought

46 million of United State citizen on Food Stamps
14 million Americans receive disability checks
Unemployment rate 14.3% ?
United States print 200 million dollars an hour
85 billion dollars a month
1 trillion dollars a year
Is this creating Inflation and devaluing our currency?
Capital Flight = Is the world looking for other currency to be the
World Reserve Currency
SDR denominated Bonds?
Start investing in and buy Gold and Silver?

I Love You Even More

As The years have gone by
And the test of time challenged our love
We wake up in the same bed every morning
Regardless if we had an argument or not
I know he loves you
But I Love you even more
I know he cares for you
But what we have is rarer than any love
I took you for dinner last night

Our 3rd anniversary celebrating our love
I gave you another diamond ring
And the waiter brought us a bottle of champagne
I know he loves you
But I Love you even more
I know he cares for you
But what we have is rarer than any love
Woman you are so beautiful to me
I can never let you go today or tomorrow
I will cherish our love forever
Like it is the last moment on this earth
I know he loves you
But I Love you even more
I know he cares for you
But what we have is rarer than any love
Today is a new day for you and me
There is no price I would not pay
Just to have you by my side
Love reside in this house and our hearts
I know he loves you
But I Love you even more
I know he cares for you
But what we have is rarer than any love

Food For Thought

en.wikipedia.org/wiki/
Natural law, or the law of nature (Latin: lex naturalis), is a system of law that is purportedly determined by nature, and thus universal.[1] Classically, natural law refers to the use of reason to analyze human nature — both social and personal — and deduce binding rules of moral behavior from it. Natural law is often contrasted with the positive law of a given political community, society, or state.[2] In legal theory, on the other hand, the interpretation of positive law requires some reference to natural law. On this understanding of natural law, natural law can be invoked to criticize judicial decisions about what the law says but not to criticize the best interpretation of the law itself. Some scholars use natural law synonymously with natural justice or natural right (Latin ius naturale),[3] while others distinguish between natural law and natural right.[1]
Although natural law is often conflated with common law, the two are distinct in that natural law is a view that certain rights or values are inherent in or universally cognizable by virtue of human reason or human nature, while common law is the legal tradition whereby certain rights or values are legally cognizable by virtue of judicial recognition or articulation.[4] Natural law theories have, however, exercised a profound influence on the development of English common law,[5][full citation needed] and have featured greatly in the philosophies of Thomas Aquinas, Francisco Suárez, Richard Hooker, Thomas Hobbes, Hugo Grotius, Samuel von Pufendorf, John Locke, Francis Hutcheson, Jean Jacques Burlamaqui, and Emmerich de Vattel. Because of the intersection between natural law and natural rights, it has been cited as a component in the United States Declaration of Independence and the Constitution of the United States, as well as in the Declaration of the Rights of Man and of the Citizen. Declarationism states that the founding of the United States is based on Natural law. Also could natural law , deal with living and eating in a natural manner. The food we eat should it be organic in nature to maximize our growth, age and brain capacity. Will the process foods and hybrid vegetables we eat today keep us from gaining entrance into the true cosmic force in our universe the brotherhood of all kind. The galaxy is full of planets and life forces

that are in tune to the good force of nature and the universe. Getting back to our nature and the natural law will heal our planet of the wrong we have committed on it and the people.

Food For Thought

Negro World was a weekly newspaper, established in 1918 in New York City, that served as the voice of the Universal Negro Improvement Association and African Communities League (UNIA), an organization founded by Marcus Garvey in 1914. Garvey founded the UNIA in July 1918 and within a few months had started publishing Negro World.[1]
The paper had a distribution of upwards of five hundred thousand copies weekly at its peak, which included both subscribers and newspaper purchasers. Monthly, the Negro World distributed more copies than The Messenger, The Crisis and Opportunity (other important African-American publications). Colonial rulers banned its sales and even possession in their territories, including both British[1] and French[2] possessions. Distribution in foreign countries was conducted through black seamen who would smuggle the paper into such areas. It ceased publication in 1933.
For a nickel, readers received a front-page editorial by Garvey, along with poetry and articles of international interest to people of African ancestry. Under the editorship of Amy Jacques the paper featured a full page called, "Our Women and What They Think". The Negro World also played an important part in the Harlem Renaissance (or Jazz Age) of the 1920s. It was a focal point for publication on the arts and African-American culture, including poetry,[3] commentary on theatre and music, and regular book reviews. Romeo Lionel Dougherty, a prominent figure of the jazz age, began writing for the Negro World in 1922.[4]

Food For Thought

Charles Hamilton Houston (September 3, 1895 – April 22, 1950) was a prominent African-American lawyer, Dean of Howard University Law School, and NAACP Litigation Director who played a significant role in dismantling the Jim Crow laws, which earned him the title "The Man Who Killed Jim Crow".[1] He is also well known for having trained future Supreme Court Justice Thurgood Marshall. Houston was born in Washington, D.C. His father worked as a lawyer. Houston started at Amherst College in 1911, was elected to the Phi Beta Kappa honor society,[3] and graduated as valedictorian in 1915. He returned to D.C. to teach at Howard University. As the U.S. entered World War I, Houston joined the then racially segregated U. S. Army as an officer and was sent to France. He returned to the U.S. in 1919, and began attending Harvard Law School. He was a member of the Harvard Law Review and graduated cum laude.

Through his work at the NAACP, Houston played a role in nearly every civil rights case before the Supreme Court between 1930 and Brown v. Board of Education (1954). Houston's plan to attack and defeat Jim Crow segregation by demonstrating the inequality in the "separate but equal" doctrine from the Supreme Court's Plessy v. Ferguson decision as it pertained to public education in the United States was the masterstroke that brought about the landmark Brown decision. Houston died from a heart attack on April 22, 1950 at the age of 54. [4] He was posthumously awarded the NAACP's Spingarn Medal in 1950 and, in 1958, the main building of the Howard University School of Law was dedicated as Charles Hamilton Houston Hall. His significance became more broadly known through the success of Thurgood Marshall and after the 1983 publication of Genna Rae McNeil's Groundwork: Charles Hamilton Houston and the Struggle for Civil Rights. Per wikepdia

Food For Thought

In 2007 President George W. Bush established AFRICOM, a unified command for U.S. military forces in Africa. George said the command was set up for peaceful reasons. Military aid and questionable trade, have been the twin pillars of America's involvement in Africa. Imperial acquisition (or the acquisition of natural resources), according to crossedcrocodiles.com "masquerades" as humanitarian aid and manifests as the militarization of the continent through the U.S. Africa Command, AFRICOM.

A quote from AL Hajji Robert J Rowland, African (Kemitic) people where ever you reside on earth you are to be aware that Africa is the cradle of civilization. Africa should be united with a president, a Governor over each country, representative from each country establishing laws and economic system for the survival of the Continent. Africa is rich in diamonds, gold, oil, trees, bauxite, uranium, aluminum, natural gas and etc. outside forces are manipulating and are the backbone of corruption and warfare on our continent. From the Organization of African Unity, to the modern day African Union, Africa must unite.

Famous Quotes

Goals: There's no telling what you can do when you get inspired by them. There's no telling what you can do when you believe in them. There's no telling what will happen when you act upon them.
— Jim Rohn

"How old would you be if you didn't know how old you are?"
— Satchel Paige

Start where you are. Distant fields always look greener, but opportunity lies right where you are. Take advantage of every opportunity of service.
— Robert J. Collier

"To keep the body in good health is a duty... otherwise we shall not be able to keep our mind strong and clear."
— Buddha

A person is not given integrity. It results from the relentless pursuit of honesty at all times.
— Unknown

"Identify your problems but give your power and energy to solutions."
— Tony Robbins

Do the things you used to talk about doing but never did. Know when to let go and when to hold on tight. Stop rushing. Don't be intimidated to say it like it is. Stop apologizing all the time. Learn to say no, so your yes has some oomph. Spend time with the friends who lift you up, and cut loose the ones who bring you down. Stop giving your power away. Be more concerned with being interested than being interesting. Be old enough to appreciate your freedom, and young enough to enjoy it. Finally know who you are.
— Kristin Armstrong

"People, even more than things, have to be restored, renewed, revived, reclaimed, and redeemed; never throw out anyone."
— Audrey Hepburn

Always dream and shoot higher than you know you can do. Don't bother just to be better than your contemporaries or predecessors. Try to be better than yourself.
— William Faulkner

"A little girl and her father were crossing a bridge. The father was kind of scared so he asked his little daughter: "Sweetheart, please hold my hand so that you don't fall into the river."
The little girl said: "No, Dad. You hold my hand."
"What's the difference?" Asked the puzzled father.
"There's a big difference," replied the little girl.
"If I hold your hand and something happens to me, chances are that I may let your hand go. But if you hold my hand, I know for sure that no matter what happens, you will never let my hand go."
In any relationship, the essence of trust is not in its bind, but in its bond. So hold the hand of the person whom you love rather than expecting them to hold yours..."
— Unknown

"The truth is that the more intimately you know someone, the more clearly you'll see their flaws. That's just the way it is. This is why marriages fail, why children are abandoned, why friendships don't last. You might think you love someone until you see the way they act when they're out of money or under pressure or hungry, for goodness' sake. Love is something different. Love is choosing to serve someone and be with someone in spite of their filthy heart. Love is patient and kind, love is deliberate. Love is hard. Love is pain and sacrifice, it's seeing the darkness in another person and defying the impulse to jump ship."
— Unknown

I have found the paradox that if I love until it hurts, then there is no hurt, but only more love.
— Mother Teresa

"The function of education is to teach one to think intensively and to think critically. Intelligence plus character - that is the goal of true education."
— Martin Luther King, Jr.

The beautiful thing about learning is that no one can take it away from you.
— B. B. King

"Anyone can give up, it's the easiest thing in the world to do. But to hold it together when everyone else would understand if you fell apart, that's true strength."
— Unknown

To love means loving the unlovable. To forgive means pardoning the unpardonable. Faith means believing the unbelievable. Hope means hoping when everything seems hopeless.
— G. K. Chesterton

Do the things you used to talk about doing but never did. Know when to let go and when to hold on tight. Stop rushing. Don't be intimidated to say it like it is. Stop apologizing all the time. Learn to say no, so your yes has some oomph. Spend time with the friends who lift you up, and cut loose the ones who bring you down. Stop giving your power away. Be more concerned with being interested than being interesting. Be old enough to appreciate your freedom, and young enough to enjoy it. Finally know who you are.
— Kristin Armstrong

Prophet Muhammad - "The ink of the scholar is more holy than the blood of a martyr."

Food For Thought

Just because I do not believe in God the way you believe in God. I respect your belief because God has inspire all the tribes on the planet and throughout the Universe. Inside of you there is a soul that connects each and every one of us to the cosmic commonality and purpose of our being. Mankind there is a battle of Good versus Evil, you have a choice what ever your color might be. Look inside your heart and feel the beat of life, we are the same but our differences are geographical locations, customs, cultural, nationalities, language, religions and political structures. The gathering is around the corner on your next stop. What road did you take to get here, I hope the good one.

Al Hajji Robert J. Rowland

Miss Hazel

We lost another soul on earth
But heaven gains a new spirit for the ages
She was a mother who raised her children
Giving them love and affection
Now she is on her way home
To be with the Angels above
There will be tears of sorrow and tears of joy
That she does not have to go through the pain anymore
My friend God will give you strength to carry on
You were with her in her time of need
The nurse, the daughter, the friend and companion
You will never forget her she will always be with you
All praises are due to God
I pray He keeps hands on you!

Dedicated to Sharon Odom, May God be with you

Tata Madiba

Warriors come and Warriors go
Children have died for freedom
Hoping to unite difference of men
Your gang, Your tribe, Your faith, Your color, My color
How much oppression can a soul take?
What was the difference between Apartheid and Jim Crow?
No man has superiority over another.
The Shadow follows everybody when the light reflects it.
Peace and harmony is the message God left the ancient ones.
Get on board the Train of Justice, Peace, Love, Wisdom, Truth
And Maat will Return, Reconciliation and Fulfillment.

Dedicated to Nelson Mandela

Al Hajji Robert J. Rowland

From Wikipedia Agenda 21 and MK Ultra

Agenda 21 is it the master plan of the New World Order for the 21st century or just a plan for Humankind to wake up and lived together and saved our planet. This is just a glimpse of the Agenda 21.
The world's leading experts in all the relevant fields agree that Humankind now has the ... plans in place: more than 1,800 local authorities in 31 countries have developed Local. Agenda 21 actions plans for sustainable development
United Nations Conference on Environment & Development
Rio De Janerio, Brazil, 3 to 14 June 1992
AGENDA 21
 Agenda 21 is a non-binding, voluntarily implemented action plan of the United Nations with regard to sustainable development. [1] It is a product of the UN Conference on Environment and Development (UNCED) held in Rio de Janeiro, Brazil, in 1992. It is an action agenda for the UN, other multilateral organizations, and individual governments around the world that can be executed at local, national, and global levels. The "21" in Agenda 21 refers to the 21st Century. It has been affirmed and modified at subsequent UN conferences.
Agenda 21 is a 300-page document divided into 40 chapters that have been grouped into 4 sections:
Section I: Social and Economic Dimensions is directed toward combatting poverty, especially in developing countries, changing consumption patterns, promoting health, achieving a more sustainable population, and sustainable settlement in decision making.
Section II: Conservation and Management of Resources for Development Includes atmospheric protection, combating deforestation, protecting fragile environments, conservation of biological diversity (biodiversity), control of pollution and the management of biotechnology, and radioactive wastes.
Section III: Strengthening the Role of Major Groups includes the roles of children and youth, women, NGOs, local authorities, business and industry, and workers; and strengthening the role of indigenous peoples, their communities, and farmers.
Section IV: Means of Implementation: implementation includes science, technology transfer, education, international institutions and

financial mechanisms.

Agenda 21 spreads it tentacles from Governments, to federal and local authorities, and right down to community groups. Chapter 28 of Agenda 21 specifically calls for each community to formulate its own Local Agenda 21: "Each local authority should enter into a dialogue with its citizens, local organizations, and private enterprises to formulate 'a Local Agenda 21.' Through consultation and consensus-building, local authorities would learn from citizens and from local, civic, community, business and industrial organizations and acquire the information needed for formulating the best strategies." - Agenda 21, Chapter 28, sec 1.3

https://www.princeton.edu/.../Project_MKULTRA.ht...Princeton University

Is project MK Ultra still going on here is a glimpse of what has been happening!

Project MK Ultra is the code name of an illegal U.S. government human research operation experimenting in the behavioral engineering of humans through the CIA's Scientific Intelligence Division. The program began in the early 1950s, was officially sanctioned in 1953, was reduced in scope in 1964, further curtailed in 1967 and officially halted in 1973.[1] The program engaged in many illegal activities;[2][3][4] in particular it used unwitting U.S. and Canadian citizens as its test subjects, which led to controversy regarding its legitimacy.[2](p74)[5][6][7] MK Ultra used numerous methodologies to manipulate people's mental states and alter brain functions, including the surreptitious administration of drugs (especially LSD) and other chemicals, hypnosis, sensory deprivation, isolation, verbal and sexual abuse, as well as various forms of torture.[8]

The scope of Project MK Ultra was broad, with research undertaken at 80 institutions, including 44 colleges and universities, as well as hospitals, prisons and pharmaceutical companies. [9] The CIA operated through these institutions using front organizations, although sometimes top officials at these institutions were aware of the CIA's involvement. [10] As the Supreme Court later noted, MK ULTRA was:

concerned with "the research and development of chemical, biological, and radiological materials capable of employment in clandestine operations to control human behavior." The program consisted of some 149 subprojects which the Agency contracted out to various universities, research foundations, and similar institutions. At least 80 institutions and 185 private researchers participated. Because the Agency funded MK ULTRA indirectly, many of the participating individuals were unaware that they were dealing with the Agency. [11]

Project MK Ultra was first brought to public attention in 1975 by the Church Committee of the U.S. Congress, and a Gerald Ford commission to investigate CIA activities within the United States. Investigative efforts were hampered by the fact that CIA Director Richard Helms ordered all MK Ultra files destroyed in 1973; the Church Committee and Rockefeller Commission investigations relied on the sworn testimony of direct participants and on the relatively small number of documents that survived Helms' destruction order. [12]

In 1977, a Freedom of Information Act request uncovered a cache of 20,000 documents relating to project MK Ultra, which led to Senate hearings later that same year. [2] In July 2001 some surviving information regarding MK Ultra was officially declassified.

Ancient Kemetic Philosophy on the Human Body and Soul

Thus we have seen the whole man. Consisted of a Natural Body a Spiritual Body, a Heart, a Double, a Soul, a Shadow, an intangible ethereal casing or Spirit, A Form, a Name. All these were however bound together inseparably, and the welfare of any Single one of them concerned the welfare of all. (From the Egyptian Book of the Dead)

Khat= Physical Body of man considered as a whole.

Sahu (Spiritual Body)

Khat changes into the Sahu by the prayers and ceremonies on the day of burial, have such phases

1. I germinate like the plants
2. My flesh germinate
3. I exist, I exist, I live, I live
4. Thy soul liveth, thy body germinate by the command of Ra(Neter, Meter, Amon, Aten, Allah, God) My Sahu has the power of associating with the soul and of holding converse with it. In this form it can ascend into heaven and dwell with the Gods and the Sahu of the Gods.

Ab = Heart

The seat of power of life and the fountain of good and evil thoughts

KA = Double

Meaning Image, Genius double, Character, disposition and mental attributes

Sekhem = Image

Prophet = Am Su ?

Ba=Soul

Meaning Ba is no incorporeal for although it dwells in the Ka and is in some respect like the heart, the principle of life in man, possesses both substance and form, in form the Kamites (Egyptian) depicted it as a human headed hawk and in nature and substance it is stated to be exceedingly refined or ethereal (very light airy, delicate, not earthly, heavenly, celestial)The Ba can revisit the body in the tomb and reanimated it an converse with it. Take upon it self any shape. Could decay if not properly nourished . Permanent dwelling place of the Ba or Soul is heaven with the Gods. Whose life it shares.

Tuat=Abode of the dead

Kemetic (Egyptian) under world, Gods of the dead and departed souls. Souls of the dead made their way in the other world by a ladder according to a ancient view, or through a gap in the mountain of Abydos called Peka. Which ever way they passed from earth, their destination was a region in Tuat.

Khaibit = Shadow of the man
Was a part of the human economy supposed to have entirely independent existence and be able to separate itself from body, free to move wherever it pleased.

Khu=Intelligence
A shining or translucent (letting light pass through but not transparent(to see through)
Intangible casing or covering of the body. Frequently depicted in the form of a mummy. Translated shining ones, glorious, intelligence, but in certain cases it may be tolerably well be rendered as spirit. The khus of the Gods lived in Heaven and also the Khus of man.

Sekhem=Form
Meaning power, form it is connected with the Ba(soul) and **Khu**(intellect)

Ren=Name
The name of a man was believed to exist in Heaven and in the Pyramid texts we are told that Neferen Al Hajji Omowalle Alif Abdul Rakiem Pen Hena Ren Fanx Al Hajji Pen hena kaf

Happy is Al Hajji Omowalle Alif Abdul Rakiem with his name Liveth Al Hajji with his Ka

Ancient Kamites (Egyptian) worship one God the hidden one. He was nameless, incomprehensible, and internal. Amun, Neter, Amon, Aten, Amen were they his or her name? Primeval matter which contained everything in embryo, the matter was water (NU) which they deified (to make God like) and everything which rose there from was a God.

<u>Neter</u> = Great supreme powers, which made the earth, the heavens the sea, the sky, men and women, animals, birds, and creeping things. All that is and all that shall be.

<u>Neteru</u> = Gods amongst these must be included the great cosmic powers and the beings who, although hold to be super natural, were yet finite and mortal, and were endowed by the Kamites (Egyptian) with love, hatred, and passion of every sort and kind.

Paut Neteru = company of the Gods

Paut Aat = The great company of the Gods

Paut Neteset = The lesser company of the Gods

Ankh = Issis the holder of the Ba (soul), The reviver of life, The transformer of life, the healer of the sick, It can raise the dead.

The Ancient Kamites (Egyptians) had master Quantum Entanglement
Telepathic communication with the Gods and themselves, through Prayer, Meditation, exercise, and Love.

Maat =Truth, Justice, Peace, Wisdom and Love.

Najm = Or The Star

I saw a face that brought back memories

Even though she was a friend

My heart began to flutter

The mind was missing a beat

How time seems to fly by

Some people you miss and you wonder why

Dreaming gets into the way of reality

Life takes you away to a path of your destiny

Love holds the key to the mystery of love

Friendship can be everlasting because lustfulness

Never got into the way of communicating

The alignment of the stars, the times, let me see you again.

Dedicated to Yvette La Fleur

Ascending

My Soul beamed into the Orion Galaxy

I was on a space boat that was full of love

I saw you standing there looking at me

We conversed with the others and the Souls of the Gods

And in our abode in Alnilam we found peace

I looked down upon the planet earth

My God it was a raging fire or was it hell?

Juba

Juba South Sudan, ethnic cleansing in Sudan, as the North versus the South
A war was going on over controlling the oil fields, gold mines and diamond mines.
Senseless killings of human beings, why can't people live in peace?
Why does war and the devil run some people Lives?
A black on black war, Sudanese fighting each other.
How can we deny the soul of our ancestor to rest in peace?
Colonialism was set up to divide Kemit (Africa).
When will Kemitic (African) people understand they were the architect of civilization?
Building pyramids, hospital, temples to the Gods, written languages and living in peace.
Now we are so lost from our true nature.
We killed each other all over our world.
Drug wars, gang wars, ethnic cleansing wars, religious wars all man made.
Peace is in God's plan, let there be peace in Sudan.

Your Gift Will Make Room For You

They say she was pretty and fine
And the young lady became a model.
This kid could hit a baseball, and one day,
He was playing for the San Francisco Giants.
Another young man and woman were scholars,
And they went to Harvard and became Lawyers.

Your Gift will make room for you.
The stars and the planets in your house
While you are in the womb.
If fed with the proper knowledge and food
The divine destiny of God will plan your future.

This child was brilliant in math
And the next thing you know he was a mechanical engineer.
How about the children who kept their heads to the sky
They became astronauts and were pilots of the space shuttle.
And the children who ask questions about God and the Angels
They are our preachers, Imams, Rabbis, Priests and Lamas.

Your Gift will make room for you.
The stars and the planets in your house
While you are in the womb.
If fed with the proper knowledge and food
The divine destiny of God will plan your future.

Your Gift Will Make Room For You (cont)

These children loved Biology and Chemistry,
They became our doctors and healers when we get sick,
The child that loved History and seek knowledge of the past,
They became our archaeologist studying the ancient lifestyle,
And what about our kids that keep dropping out of school
Should the education system start being more inclusive of all
Nationalities?

Your Gift will make room for you.
The stars and the planets in your house
While you are in the womb.
If fed with the proper knowledge and food
The divine destiny of God will plan your future.

This child adored music, writing and drawing
They became our novelist, artist, musician, singers and poets,
These children loved people and believe in God
And they became soldiers in war
To protect corporate greed of their country of origin
Some of these children just love life and wanted to survive
They became workers and learned a trade to get by.

Your Gift will make room for you.
The stars and the planets in your house
While you are in the womb.
If fed with the proper knowledge and food
The divine destiny of God will plan your future.

Nannyism

A whistling woman and a crowing hen,
Comes to know good end.

She thought he was the cat meow

Don't open up another door till you
Close the one you are with.

And please close the window before
You open up another window.

Please have these babies for yourself
I don't want to raise any more kids

The rich get richer and the poor get pregnant.

You are mistreating the hand that is taking care of you

Love has no time, no age, it is just right there

" She saw you but she did not see you"

Isa (Jesus Said)

"I took my stand in the midst of the world,
And in the flesh I appeared to them.
I found them all drunk, and I did not find
Any of them thirsty. My soul ached for the
children of humanity, because they are blind
in their hearts and do not see, for they came into
the world empty, and they also seek to depart
from the world empty. But mean while they are drunk,
when they shake off their wine, then they will change their ways.

Gospel Of Thomas – The Nag Hammadi- codex 2

Food For Thought

Abandon the search of God and the creation and other matters of a
similar sort. Look for him by taking yourself as the starting point.
Learn who it is within you who makes everything his own, and says
"my God, my mind, my thought, my soul, my body. "Learn the
source of sorrow, joy, love, hate, if you carefully investigate these
matters you will
Find him in your self.

"Monoimus"

Food For Thought

May the light of God shine on our souls
And may the mercy of God enveloped us
Mankind and heal us of our past transgression

Al Hajji Robert J. Rowland

Man made religions have blinded the human
Race from true brotherhood, Maat will rise again
From the primeval mound where creation began
Neter began to create and Gods and Goddess walk the earth

Al Hajji Robert J. Rowl;and

" For all there is in religion and philosophy of today
  Is what we knew in ancient Kemit (Africa)

Al Hajji Robert J. Rowland

The Indoctrination of the Fabrication of the Ancient Indigenous
Black African (Kemitic) (EGYPTIAN) on his Continent is
Antiquated and is in need of updating to Include the real
contributions that have been made by their cultural to our modern
World, In the School Rooms around the world!

Al Hajji Robert J. Rowland

My Son

My son let love be in your heart
Please forgive me for not being there every day
Do not let this world harden your heart.
God has blessed you with many gifts.
Let your fingers create songs on your guitar.
That will help change our world
And bring harmony to mankind.
I remember the day you were born.
Another part of me would be walking on this earth.
I knew God's angels were watching over you.
With focus and discipline you will be able
To do whatever you dream to be.
The road map to your life plan has been written out.
Make sure you show up each and every day and
Absorb the knowledge that this world has to offer you.
Stay on the Godly path, do not deviate to satan's plan.
Your soul is special and a good one is best of God.
Treat others the way you want to be treated.
My son let love be in your heart.

I Am Smiling

I am smiling, I got you thinking about me
I am smiling, only you and me can understand
I am smiling, God sent you to ease my pain of this world
I am smiling, you touched my tickled spot
I am smiling, love is in the air it is everywhere
I am smiling, these are tears of joy
I am smiling, I got songs to sing about life and love
I am smiling, my prayers have been answered from God the almighty within my soul
I am smiling, your beauty is right before my eyes
I am smiling, I got to hear your voice today.
I am smiling, love is one beat away from my heart
I am smiling, my wife to be loves God and all the prophets he sent us
I am smiling, the black ancient Kemitic (Egyptians) are finally being recognized
I am smiling, angels are watching over our family members my Queen
I am smiling, thinking with my conscious and controlling my emotions
I am smiling, I do not dwell in the past very long I just keep moving on

Inside Of You

I was sitting home all alone and
I didn't know what I was going to do
Wondering if love would ever come my way again
I prayed to God every day to give me patience
And send me my soul mate the one just for me

Inside of you, love came within the night
Inside of you, dreams can come true
Inside of you, became all the joys and delights
Inside of you, our souls met and we became one

I laid down one night and closed my eyes
Your face appeared in my thoughts and
Then I saw you under the plane at TSU
I walked through the door and there you were
I wondered how could I approach you
And let you know who I am
And then we were on Nanny's couch one night
Talking and trying to figure us out.

Inside of you, love came within the night
Inside of you, dreams can come true
Inside of you, became all the joys and delights
Inside of you, our souls met and we became one

I bought some orchids the kind that will never die
I looked and the clock was ticking time
And time honey was on our side
Will I wake and this moment be just a dream?
But I am touching you and holding you
And inside of you; this must be for real baby

Inside of you, love came within the night
Inside of you, dreams can come true
Inside of you, became all the joys and delights
Inside of you, our souls met and we became one

Ancient Kemitic (Egyptian) Proverbs

Egyptian Proverbs were a very important part of the Ancient religion of Egypt, one of the main religious concepts the Egyptians had was "know yourself." Their spiritual aspect of this concept held that within man is the divine essence of the Creator and the heavens. And this finds expression in their teaching: "The kingdom of heaven is within you; and whosoever shall know himself shall find it.". Proverbs were held as a teaching method for a man to understand the universe, thus they were inscribed in temples and tombs of Egypt, these inscriptions might be the first Holy Book known by man.

Below are some of the powerful teachings proverbs found in the temples of Luxor.

- The best and shortest road towards knowledge of truth is Nature.
- For every joy there is a price to be paid.
- If his heart rules him, his conscience will soon take the place of the rod.
- What you are doing does not matter so much as what you are learning from doing it? It is better not to know and to know that one does not know, than presumptuously to attribute some random meaning to symbols.
- If you search for the laws of harmony, you will find knowledge.
- If you are searching for a Neter, observe Nature!
Exuberance is a good stimulus towards action, but the inner light grows in silence and concentration.
- Not the greatest Master can go even one step for his disciple; in himself he must experience each stage of developing consciousness. Therefore, he will know nothing for which he is not ripe.
- The body is the house of god. That is why it is said, "Man know yourself."

- True teaching is not an accumulation of knowledge; it is an awaking of consciousness which goes through successive stages.
- The man who knows how to lead one of his brothers towards what he has known may one day be saved by that very brother.

- People bring about their own undoing through their tongues.
- If one tries to navigate unknown waters one runs the risk of shipwreck.
- Leave him in error who loves his error.
- Every man is rich in excuses to safeguard his prejudices, his instincts, and his opinions.
- To know means to record in one's memory; but to understand means to blend with the thing and to assimilate it oneself.
- There are two kinds of error: blind credulity and piecemeal criticism. Never believe a word without putting its truth to the test; discernment does not grow in laziness; and this faculty of discernment is indispensable to the Seeker. Sound skepticism is the necessary condition for good discernment; but piecemeal criticism is an error.
- Love is one thing, knowledge is another.
- True sages are those who give what they have, without meanness and without secret!
- An answer brings no illumination unless the question has matured to a point where it gives rise to this answer which thus becomes its fruit. Therefore, learn how to put a question.
- What reveals itself to me ceases to be mysterious for me alone: if I unveil it to anyone else, he hears mere words which betray the living sense: Profanation, but never revelation.
- The first concerning the 'secrets': all cognition comes from inside; we are therefore initiated only by ourselves, but the Master gives the keys.
- The second concerning the 'way': the seeker has need of a Master to guide him and lift him up when he falls, to lead him back to the right way when he strays.
- Understanding develops by degrees.
- As to deserving, know that the gift of heaven is free; this gift of Knowledge is so great that no effort whatever could hope to 'deserve' it.
- If the Master teaches what is error, the disciple's submission is slavery; if he teaches truth, this submission is ennoblement.
- There grows no wheat where there is no grain.
- The only thing that is humiliating is helplessness.
- An answer if profitable in proportion to the intensity of the quest.
- Listen to your conviction, even if they seem absurd to your reason.

-- Know the world in yourself. Never look for yourself in the world, for this would be to project your illusion

To teach one must know the nature of those whom one is teaching.

- In every vital activity it is the path that matters.
- The way of knowledge is narrow.
- Each truth you learn will be, for you, as new as if it had never been written.
- The only active force that arises out of possession is fear of losing the object of possession.
- If you defy an enemy by doubting his courage you double it.
- The nut doesn't reveal the tree it contains.
- For knowledge... you should know that peace is an indispensable condition of getting it.
- The first thing necessary in teaching is a master; the second is a pupil capable of carrying on the tradition.
- Peace is the fruit of activity, not of sleep.
- Envious greed must govern to possess and ambition must possess to govern.
- When the governing class isn't chosen for quality it is chosen for material wealth: this always means decadence; the lowest stage a society can reach.
-
- One foot isn't enough to walk with.
- Our senses serve to affirm, not to know.
- We mustn't confuse mastery with mimicry, knowledge with superstitious ignorance.
- Physical consciousness is indispensable for the achievement of knowledge.
- A man can't be judge of his neighbor' intelligence. His own vital experience is never his neighbor's.
- No discussion can throw light if it wanders from the real point.
- Your body is the temple of knowledge.
- Experience will show you, a Master can only point the way.

-- A house has the character of the man who lives in it.
- All organs work together in the functioning of the whole.
- A man's heart is his own Neter.
- A pupil may show you by his own efforts how much he deserves to

learn from you.
- Routine and prejudice distort vision. Each man thinks his own horizon is the limit of the world.
- You will free yourself when you learn to be neutral and follow the instructions of your heart without letting things perturb you. This is the way of Maat.
- Judge by cause, not by effect.
- Growth in consciousness doesn't depend on the will of the intellect or its possibilities but on the intensity of the inner urge.
- Every man must act in the rhythm of his time... such is wisdom.
- Men need images. Lacking them they invent idols. Better then to found the images on realities that lead the true seeker to the source.
- Maat, who links universal to terrestrial, the divine with the human is incomprehensible to the cerebral intelligence.
- Have the wisdom to abandon the values of a time that has passed and pick out the constituents of the future. An environment must be suited to the age and men to their environment.
- Everyone finds himself in the world where he belongs. The essential thing is to have a fixed point from which to check its reality now and then.
- Always watch and follow nature.

-- A phenomenon always arises from the interaction of complementary. If you want something look for the complement that will elicit it. Seth causes Horus.
H Horus redeems Seth.
- All seed answer light, but the color is different.
- The plant reveals what is in the seed.
- Popular beliefs on essential matters must be examined in order to discover the original thought.
- It is the passive resistance from the helm that steers the boat.
- The key to all problems is the problem of consciousness.
- Man must learn to increase his sense of responsibility and of the fact that everything he does will have its consequences.
- If you would build something solid, don't work with wind: always look for a fixed point, something you know that is stable... yourself.
- If you would know yourself, take yourself as starting point and go back to its source; your beginning will disclose your end.
- Images are nearer reality than cold definitions.

- Seek peacefully, you will find.
- Organization is impossible unless those who know the laws of harmony lay the foundation.
- It is no use whatever preaching Wisdom to men: you must inject it into their blood.
- Knowledge is consciousness of reality. Reality is the sum of the laws that govern nature and of the causes from which they flow.
- Social good is what brings peace to family and society.
- Knowledge is not necessarily wisdom.
- By knowing one reaches belief. By doing one gains conviction. When you know, dare.
- Altruism is the mark of a superior being.
- All is within yourself. Know your most inward self and look for what corresponds with it in nature.
- The seed cannot sprout upwards without simultaneously sending roots into the ground.
- The seed includes all the possibilities of the tree.... The seed will develop these possibilities, however, only if it receives corresponding energies from the sky.
- Grain must return to the earth, die, and decompose for new growth to begin.
- Man, know yourself... and you shalt know the gods.

Works Citied

Inspirational Quote, Inspirational daily@weblandmail.com

Thoughtful mind Quotes@thoughtful-mind.com

"Wikipedia "Wikipedia Atlantic Slave Trade 20 Feb 2013 <http://www.wikipedia.org

WWW.arabslavetrade.com designed via African Code

Crossedcrocodilies.com

THE BOOK OF THE DEAD The Papyrus of Ani by E. A. WALLIS BUDGE (1895) www.hermetics.org/pdf/sacred/BookOfDead.pdf by EAW BUDGE -)2/03/2014

Hillard III, G.Asa, Williams, Larry & Damali, Nia: The Teaching of Ptahhotep, The Oldest Book in the World. Atlanta, GA. Blackwood Press

Wikipedia web site www.wikipedia.org

http://www.aldokkan.com/art/proverbs.htm

The Nag Hammadi. Library www.ebook3000.com/the-nag-libraryhammadi-library_10195-0

www.ingramcontent.com/pod-product-compliance
Lightning Source LLC
Chambersburg PA
CBHW020948030426
42339CB00004B/4